THE DIVINE COMEDY
TRACING GOD'S ART

TWAYNE'S MASTERWORK STUDIES
ROBERT LECKER, GENERAL EDITOR

ADVENTURES OF HUCKLEBERRY FINN: AMERICAN COMIC VISION
by David E. E. Sloane
ANIMAL FARM: PASTORALISM AND POLITICS by Richard I. Smyer
THE BIBLE: A LITERARY STUDY by John H. Gottcent
THE BIRTH OF TRAGEDY: A COMMENTARY by David Lenson
THE CANTERBURY TALES: A LITERARY PILGRIMAGE by David Williams
DUBLINERS: A PLURALISTIC WORLD by Craig Hansen Werner
GREAT EXPECTATIONS: A NOVEL OF FRIENDSHIP by Bert G. Hornback
HEART OF DARKNESS: SEARCH FOR THE UNCONSCIOUS by Gary Adelman
THE INTERPRETATION OF DREAMS: FREUD'S THEORIES REVISITED
by Laurence M. Porter
INVISIBLE MAN: RACE AND IDENTITY by Kerry McSweeney
JANE EYRE: PORTRAIT OF A LIFE by Maggie Berg
MADAME BOVARY: THE END OF ROMANCE by Eric Gans
MIDDLEMARCH: A NOVEL OF REFORM by Bert G. Hornback
MOBY-DICK: ISHMAEL'S MIGHTY BOOK by Kerry McSweeney
ONE FLEW OVER THE CUCKOO'S NEST: RISING TO HEROISM by M. Gilbert Porter
PARADISE LOST: IDEAL AND TRAGIC EPIC by Francis C. Blessington
PRIDE AND PREJUDICE: A STUDY IN ARTISTIC ECONOMY by Kenneth L. Moler
THE RED BADGE OF COURAGE: REDEFINING THE HERO by Donald B. Gibson
THE SCARLET LETTER: A READING by Nina Baym
SONS AND LOVERS: A NOVEL OF DIVISION AND DESIRE by Ross C Murfin
THE STRANGER: HUMANITY AND THE ABSURD by English Showalter, Jr.
THE SUN ALSO RISES: A NOVEL OF THE TWENTIES by Michael S. Reynolds
THE TURN OF THE SCREW: BEWILDERED VISION by Terry Heller
TO THE LIGHTHOUSE: THE MARRIAGE OF LIFE AND ART by Alice van Buren Kelley
THE WASTE LAND: A POEM OF MEMORY AND DESIRE by Nancy K. Gish

THE DIVINE COMEDY
Tracing God's Art

Marguerite Mills Chiarenza

Twayne Publishers • Boston
A DIVISION OF G. K. HALL & CO.

The *Divine Comedy: Tracing God's Art*
Marguerite Mills Chiarenza

Twayne's Masterwork Studies No. 25
Copyright 1989 by G. K. Hall & Co.
All rights reserved.
Published by Twayne Publishers
A Division of G. K. Hall & Co.
70 Lincoln Street
Boston, Massachusetts 02111

Copyediting supervised by Barbara Sutton
Book production by Gabrielle B. McDonald

Typeset in 10 pt. Sabon
by Compset, Inc., of Beverly, Massachusetts

Printed on permanent/durable acid-free paper
and bound in the United States of America

Library of Congress Cataloging-in-Publication Data

10 9 8 7 6 5 4 3

Chiarenza, Marguerite Mills.
    The divine comedy : tracing God's art / Marguerite Mills
Chiarenza.
        p.   cm. — (Twayne's masterwork studies ; no. 25)
    Bibliography: p.
    Includes index.
    ISBN 0-8057-7985-X (alk. paper).   ISBN 0-8057-8034-3 (pbk. : alk.
paper)
    1. Dante Alighieri, 1265–1321. Divina commedia.   I. Title.
    II. Series.
PQ4390.C596 1989
851'.1—dc19
                                                                88-30090
                                                                CIP

CONTENTS

Note on the References and Acknowledgments
Chronology: Dante's Life and Works

I	Historical Context	1
II	The Importance of the Work	6
III	Critical Reception	9

A Reading

IV	The *Inferno*	19
V	The *Purgatorio*	56
VI	The *Paradiso*	93

Notes	127
Bibliography	128
Index	135
About the author	138

NOTE ON THE REFERENCES AND ACKNOWLEDGMENTS

Choosing a translation from the many good ones available, each of which has merits but none of which is entirely satisfactory, was not easy. While prose translations preserve more of the poem's exact meaning, they seriously distort its form. Therefore, since many of the modern verse translations, often in blank or free verse, make an extra effort toward literalness, these seem generally preferable. However, the special nature of Dante's masterpiece in which the connotations of every word carry weight, makes the greater exactness of a prose translation almost indispensable, if not for the reader at least for the teacher discussing the poem's details. Guided largely by my experience in the classroom, I chose John Sinclair's prose translation (New York: Oxford University Press, 1961) as the most literal and readable. All citations are taken from this translation, with canto and line numbers given in the text. I have made a few minor changes to Sinclair's translation for instances where a slightly different choice of words makes my discussion easier for the reader to follow. My choice of translation, however, is not clearcut. Thus, I have recommended several others in the Bibliography.

I wish to express my gratitude to Keith Clifford, Stephen Rowan, and John Lepage for their generous and perceptive advice; to Pattie Kealy for her help in organizing and editing my manuscript; and to the Social Sciences and Humanities Research Council of Canada for a grant to cover my expenses.

DANTES ALLIGHERIVS FLORENTINVS

Anonymous fourteenth-century portrait of Dante. Biblioteca Nazionale, Florence. Reproduced by permission of Archivi Alinari, Firenze.

CHRONOLOGY:
DANTE'S LIFE AND WORKS

1215	Buondelmonte murdered, beginning feud between the Buondelmonti and the Amidei that will result in the introduction into Florence of the Guelf and Ghibelline factions.
1248	Frederick II attacks Florence; Guelf leaders flee the city.
1250	Frederick II dies; Guelfs return.
1251	Farinata degli Uberti and other Ghibelline leaders banished.
1260	With Farinata leading, the Ghibellines—having regrouped, sought aid from the Emperor Manfred, and tricked Florentines into coming to the Arbia River—decimate Florence's army at Montaperti and regain control of the city.
1261	Council of Empoli, at which Farinata heroically opposes the destruction of Florence.
1265	Dante born, in Florence, to the notary Alighiero Alighieri and his wife, Bella, probably the daughter of Durante degli Abati.
1266	Charles of Anjou, brother of the king of France, himself recently crowned king of Sicily and Apulia, defeats Emperor Manfred at Benevento, where Manfred dies. Tuscan exiles led by Guido Guerra are among those fighting behind Charles.
1267	Definitive exile of Ghibelline leaders. Florentine Guelfs place the city under the lordship of Charles.
1274	Dante's first meeting with Beatrice Portinari. Saint Thomas and Saint Bonaventura die.
1276	Giotto born. The poet Guido Guinicelli dies.
1278	Bella dies. Alighiero remarries Lapa soon after, with whom he has three children. The eldest, Francesco, will support his half brother throughout his exile.
1280	Geri del Bello, Alighiero's first cousin, murdered; beginning of feud between the Alighieri and the Sacchetti. Albertus Magnus dies.

1282	Approximate date of Alighiero's death. Dante becomes the head of the family.
1283	Beatrice reappears. Farinata posthumously sentenced as heretic. Approximate beginning of Brunetto's influence on Dante's studies.
1284	Charles I of Anjou dies.
1285	Probable date of Dante's arranged marriage to Gemma Donati, with whom he will have two sons, a daughter, and a fourth child, probably male.
1287	Beatrice marries Simone de' Bardi. Dante probably begins studies in Bologna and his intimate friendship with Guido Cavalcanti.
1289	Folco Portinari, Beatrice's father, dies. Florentines, supported by Charles II of Anjou, defeat Arezzo at Campaldino. Dante almost certainly participates in this victory, as well as in the Florentine victory, a few months later at Caprona, against the Pisan Ghibellines.
1290	Beatrice dies.
1294	Pietro da Morrone becomes Pope Celestine V. His abdication the same year results in the election of Benedetto Caetani to the papacy as the infamous Boniface VIII. Approximate year of the composition of the *Vita Nuova*.
1295	Dante enrolls in the wealthy Guild of Physicians and Apothecaries in order to qualify for higher offices in the government of Florence. Several minor political actions by him are recorded during this and the next year. Brunetto Latini dies. Dante meets Charles Martel, king of Hungary, in Florence. Marco Polo returns from the East.
1300	Pope Boniface VIII proclaims the Jubilee of the year 1300. Cimabue dies. Fictional year of the events of the *Divine Comedy*. Florence is divided into Black Guelfs, led by the Donati family, and White Guelfs (Dante's party), led by the Cerchi; the origin of this highly political division was a personal family feud. Dante sent as ambassador to San Gemignano. He is elected to the high office of Prior, and takes part in the decision to banish the most prominent leaders of both parties. Among those banished is Guido Cavalcanti, who becomes sick and dies during his exile. Many of Dante's future troubles arise from the unfortunate coincidence of his priorate with this period of violence and extreme bitterness in the city.
1301	In charge of streetworks of San Procolo. Votes in the Council of the Hundred against sending help to Charles II and to Boniface VIII.

1302	Sent by the Whites as ambassador to the pope. But the pope has already sent his own representative, Charles of Valois, brother of the king of France, to Florence to "bring peace" between Blacks and Whites. Charles carries out his real mission, which is to give control of the city to Blacks. During Dante's absence, Whites are exiled, he is charged with conspiracy against the pope, against the peace of the city, and against the Guelf party. Soon thereafter he is charged with corruption while in office. He is sentenced first to pay a large fine and then later to death if he re-enters the city. Exile which will last the rest of his life begins.
1303	In Verona as guest of Bartolomeo della Scala. Boniface VIII dies.
1304	In Arezzo, plots forcible re-entry with exiled Whites and some Ghibellines. Blacks have taken over all political offices in Florence. Dante opposes a hopeless attack on Florence, but he is outvoted by the great majority. The attack fails; four hundred of the exiles and their allies are killed. Dante breaks off relations with the group. Over the next three or four years he is probably working on his unfinished treatises on language and on philosophy.
1305–1307	Probable period of his stay in Lunigiana with the Malaspina family, for which he performs diplomatic services.
1308	Probably in Lucca, where his wife and children may have been residing. The leader of the Blacks, Corso Donati, is killed. Possibly begins work on the *Divine Comedy*.
1309	Possibly studies in Paris.
1311	In Italy, vehemently supports Henry VII, whose coronation in Rome he attends. Writes outspoken letter to the Florentines, reproaching and threatening them for not supporting Emperor Henry. Writes letter to Henry imploring him to attack Florence. Pardon issued by Florence to exiles, but Dante is explicitly excluded.
1312–1318	Mostly in Verona, as honored guest of Cangrande della Scala.
1312	Henry VII makes unsuccessful attack on Florence.
1313	Henry VII dies, taking Dante's political hopes with him. Boccaccio born.
1315	New condemnations of Dante, his sons, and others by Florentines.
1316	Amnesty granted to exiles who pay a fine. Dante rejects terms as degrading admission of guilt. Seems unaware that once again he is explicitly excluded from offer.

1318–1321	In Ravenna under the protection of Guido Novello da Polenta, nephew of Francesca da Rimini, where his children join him. Completes the *Divine Comedy*.
1320	Public reading in Verona of the *Quaestio de Aqua et Terra*, Dante's short physical treatise on the relation between land and water surfaces of the earth.
1321	Sent by Guido da Polenta to conduct negotiations with Venice. Becomes ill during trip and dies on his return. Guido arranges funeral with great honors. Dante buried in Ravenna, where his bones remain despite repeated attempts by Florentines to have them returned to his birthplace.

CHAPTER I

Historical Context

Our knowledge of Dante's life consists of a few facts, a larger number of unreliable stories, and a vivid but imagined sense of his personality as it is projected through his works. In other words, we speculate about the historical figure much more than we know about him. But this speculation is an important part of our interpretation of his masterpiece, in which he demands that we believe in the authenticity of a vision that is somehow the poetic version of the intense experience of his life. If properly conducted, our speculation will enhance our understanding, for it will lead us to ask ourselves questions about those things that Dante may have seen or known and the meaning they take on in his poem. It can help us to see the coherence of his great vision, to understand his message, and to appreciate the quality of the poetic imagination that is constantly transforming experience into vision.

But if our speculation is of a more gossipy sort, aimed at discovering what Dante chose not to tell us, then it will probably never enlighten our understanding of what he *did* tell us. I am thinking of interpretations that, for instance, surmise that the presence of a character in Hell is evidence of an act the poet held against him. In such cases we are using what Dante did say as the means of trying to know what he did not say. This method will lead us astray; causing us to distort the poem itself, which remains our most valuable source of knowledge about Dante as well as the reason we endeavor to know him in the first place. If, however, we use the background information we are able to obtain to understand what Dante must have meant with his poem, then not only do we clarify our reading, but we gain insight into the world he experienced so intensely as well. Dante's poem was his way of standing back from the turbulent events of his times in order to gain the perspective necessary to see inside and beyond them, not his way of participating in them. With this understood, let us look at some aspects of the world Dante lived in.

Florence, at the time of Dante's birth, was one of the most successful city-states in Italy. Art and commerce flourished under a well-conceived democratic government of representatives of the trades. But, like much of the rest of Italy, Florence was not a place of peace. Its citizens were constantly at war with each other and with neighboring cities. In the streets, gangs fought and individuals were treacherously attacked and often murdered. Near the city, bloody battles left the fields strewn with wounded and dead citizens. These hostilities were brought about by a combination of personal and political incidents. They were the more treacherous and bloody because they were personally motivated and the more costly and disruptive because of their political reverberations. Whether Guelfs and Ghibellines (Guelf and Ghibelline were labels used all over Italy by local opposing parties) or whether Black Guelfs and White Guelfs (Black and White were the names of the factions that formed within the Florentine Guelf party after it gained control of the city), the violence would typically escalate in the following way: originally, because of an insult or an act of aggression, two families would become sworn enemies; next, other families would side with one or the other enemy, forming factions; then, these factions would vie for political power within the city and fortify themselves through alliance with one or more factions in nearby cities; finally, more powerful figures, the pope or the emperor (by Dante's time "Emperor" was little more than a title of legitimacy accompanied only by the power it was able to back up militarily) would be called in to support one or another faction—the Guelfs would usually call on the pope or the king of France, the Ghibellines on the German lord then claiming imperial authority.

Dante was born just about the time that the struggles in Florence between Guelfs and Ghibellines had been resolved by the permanent exile of the most important and dangerous Ghibelline leaders. Stories told by his grandfather, Bellincione (grandson of Cacciaguida), who lived to a very old age, probably account largely for the vivid sense Dante has of this bitter period just before his birth. Dante's political career reached its peak, unhappily, just as the new struggles between Blacks and Whites broke out. Because he held high office in the government during some embittering times, his fate, like that of his family's enemies before he was born, was exile. Because of the outspoken and uncompromising positions he continued to take, his exile lasted the rest of his life. His views became increasingly hostile both to the government in power in Florence and to the pope and his allies, and increasingly favorable to imperial authority. When Henry VII descended into Italy in 1311 for his coronation as emperor, Dante rushed to his support, fervently hoping that he would seize power in all of Italy and remove the Florentine government from office. He urged the emperor to take Florence by force, but when, in fact, Henry besieged the city his attempt failed and he died before he could try again. Henry's failure marked the end of Dante's hopes for the reestablishment of effective imperial power in Italy in the foreseeable future.

Obviously Dante suffered great personal losses and indignities because of his direct involvement in the political struggles of his time. From the little we know of his life, we can say that he was politically idealistic but also fiery, agressive, and prone to advocating military solutions. He was both honored and abused during his turbulent life and was able to observe closely the complex workings of a political world of petty and greedy actions combined with ideologies of divinely ordained authority and eternally confirmed values. On the one hand, the papacy held the keys of Saint Peter and claimed the allegiance of the world. But its secular power had become so great as to eclipse its essential purpose of spiritual leadership. The ideology of Empire survived, on the other hand, in name only, for there was no effective ruler of the Empire, only many rulers of lesser kingdoms in conflict with each other. Dante witnessed, and suffered in, a world of absolute ideologies and petty practices. He did not back off from in-volvement but participated actively, gaining by his idealism and his consequent optimism, abuse, frustration, and at the same time great respect from those who appreciated the strength and honesty of his convictions and the unyielding power of his intellect. The *Divine Comedy* reflects this world and Dante's experience in it, but the pur-pose for its telling goes far beyond such a world. Its purpose is to present the vision that he acquired through his spiritual, personal, and political experience. As such, it is neither an evasion of the world nor an act of participation in it. It is aimed not at enunciating specific political goals but at communicating an urgent message of justice, and not just political justice, to humanity. The troubles of his life are not the subject of the *Divine Comedy* for the simple reason that they are small when measured beside the vision to which they have contrib-uted—a vision of justice and salvation beyond anything Dante saw on earth.

Throughout his life, even at the most turbulent moments, Dante devoted his most attentive energy to reading, meditation, and writing. The depth of his understanding of Virgil, Augustine, and Boethius alone testifies to the time and intensity he put into his reading. But the *Divine Comedy* is also a testimony to his reading and to his under-standing of countless other texts. Dante studied in Florence, where Brunetto Latini's influence on his linguistic and scientific studies must have been great, and where Cimabue and Giotto were bringing about a revolution in the visual arts; he studied in Bologna where the "sweet new style" that he named and we might say invented had just been born; and he may have studied in Paris for a brief period. If he did, this is especially important because Paris was the center of theological studies in Dante's time, which was the peak of the great age of Scho-lasticism. Whether or not Dante was ever in Paris, he was accom-plished in the subtle and not easily acquired skills of Scholastic philosophy.

Dante lived in a great age and he was its greatest representative, but perhaps nothing from his age contributed so much to his genius as the state of the literary language in Italy. Italian, as a written language, was almost newborn. Short poems or songs and religious hymns written in the dialects existed, but no major literary work had been composed in Italy in the spoken language. Short poetic experiments were ultimately imitations of similar compositions from France. But the sophisticated cities of Italy were ready for a literature of their own, and young poets were experimenting with their own dialects as the means of expressing something new. Dante meditated and wrote on the subject of the development of the spoken tongue into a literary language and his youthful experiments in the vernacular remain classics of Italian literature. The result of his study and his work was that he created the first great work of Italian literature, and his native Tuscan dialect became what we now call standard Italian.

Dante's political career is important, his intellectual career even more important. About Dante's day-to-day life we know next to nothing, because he tells us nothing. Dante considered this area private in the sense that it was, in his thinking, meaningful only to him, his family, and his close friends. But his spiritual life, his quest for Beatrice, is another matter. It is what he considered most important to others, the particular form in him of the universal feelings and desires found in every human life, whether that life triumphed through them or betrayed them.

CHAPTER II

The Importance of the Work

It is hardly worth asking whether the *Divine Comedy* is important. The countless translations (literally hundreds in English alone), commentaries (at least four within four years of the poet's death), editions (incalculable: between four and five hundred *known* manuscripts; about four hundred Italian editions); not to speak of the honors and praise that have accompanied Dante, with no serious lapse over a period of almost seven hundred years, from his death to this day, testify sufficiently to his work's importance. But we might well ask why Dante is so important and what it is that makes him so great that many would say he has no equal. There are, no doubt, as many answers to the question as there are admirers of the *Divine Comedy*. As I might formulate the undefinable quality of his poetry, Dante's genius dawns on the reader first through the strength and purity of his language. Thankfully, although much is lost, much is also preserved in translation. Dante's words seem to be saying exactly what he means, never wavering the slightest bit from his purpose. The reader senses passion in the verses. Not the passion of personal emotions, but the passion of the intensity of the poet's effort to drive his words toward their goal. What first attracts us to Dante is the sense that all of his strength is directed toward delivering a message that, in his mind at least, is of awesome importance.

The reader, sensing so strongly that the words he is reading say what they mean, tries to understand that meaning and the more effort he puts into understanding and interpreting the words, the more clarity and coherence he finds there. But the very clarity he finds only reveals more complexity. Paradoxically, the reader does not feel that the poem becomes more and more complicated as he knows it better, only that its meaning never seems to be exhausted. The thousands of interpretations of lines or parts of the *Divine Comedy* reflect the effect that the poem has had on so many readers who, initially struck by the language itself, were ultimately amazed by the richness of its message. Dante's words derive their power from their meaning; they never decorate it. We read his poetry as he read Creation, whose beauty, in his mind, was inseparable from its significance.

Dante's penetrating insights and his deep and thoughtful study of them are not a small part of his genius. But his intuition into the nature of language is unmatched. He found that the spoken language we learn from our mothers, the language we use in our lives, is the only one through which we can express experience. In Dante's day Latin, the language in which philosophers and tragic poets wrote, was considered the only suitable language for serious concepts. But Dante chose to write his massive work in his spoken tongue, which had never been used for a subject so weighty or a work of such scope. He made this important choice after concluding that, while it was possible to make his spoken language express complex concepts, it was not possible to make the language of his studies express his life, his experience. Perhaps Dante's deep awareness of the unique expressive power of his mother tongue contributed to making him the greatest "craftsman" of it. His ability to make words, sounds, and rhythms do what he wants them to do verges on the miraculous. He makes us follow a fainting body to the ground with the sound of his words (*"come corpo morto cade"*), or hear the gentle rippling of the sea (*"il tremolar della marina"*); he grates on our ear as he calls on "harsh and grating rhymes" (*"le rime aspre e chiocce"*); Francesca's sweet and gentle sounds (*"Amor ch'a nullo amato amar perdona"*) contrast with the hostility in the pilgrim's voice as he torments Filippo Argenti (*"ma tu chi se', che si se' fatto brutto"*); Dante accustoms our ear to the sound of the slow unfolding of events in time (*"La contingenza che fuor del quaderno della vostra matera non si stende"*), and then, through the sudden rapidity of the next verse, superimposes on that sound the sense of their simultaneous presence in the mind of God (*"tutta è dipinta nel cospetto etterno"*); he lends religious elevation to Aristotle's prime mover in the opening sounds of the *Paradiso* (*"La gloria di colui che tutto move"*). Although Dante's language cannot be fully appreciated in translation, much comes through even in English, for he is a craftsman of images and characters and tones as well as of sounds and rhythms.

Despite Dante's extraordinary artistry, he does not have a personal style by which to identify him. Like the virtuoso's, his style cannot be distinguished from his ability to use the instrument of language to its full potential. But, while the virtuoso exhibits his art as an end in itself, Dante places his at the service of his message. His poetic personality is that of a prophet; his belief, that his gift was bestowed on him so that he could show humanity what he had seen. Because of this, we might say Dante found rather than composed his verses, whose close relation to their message seems comparable only to that of natural beauty to its function.

CHAPTER III

Critical Reception

From the time that it was written to this day, the *Divine Comedy* has never lost its audience of fascinated readers and busy critics. The proliferation of commentaries and readings around Dante's poem testifies to the almost universal belief that it is a masterpiece and illustrates the widely held assumption that it is allegorical—that it has meanings other than the literal one. The commentaries are, in fact, dedicated in large part to elucidating the poet's "other meanings." But it is here that the consensus breaks down, both with regard to what these meanings are and with regard to what the nature of this allegory is. It is a tribute to Dante that so many have wanted to understand and interpret, even to "solve" him. However, amidst the thousands of hypotheses, there are still no exhaustive or definitive answers. This is more than a tribute to Dante: it is a demonstration of his genius. The exegeses of the *Divine Comedy* have grown over the centuries to the point where a lifetime would not suffice to read even the easily available writings on the subject. This is a phenomenon unique in the history of literary works, but not in that of sacred texts.

The earliest commentaries, two of them by Dante's sons, remain the most valuable to us. Their ability to recognize immediately the historical and cultural allusions makes them a priceless source for our studies, despite their authors' limitations as interpreters and their failures sometimes even as providers of information. Through the centuries scholars have researched every detail of the poem, adding pieces

9

of useful or useless information about words, sources, characters, or philosophical concepts to the glosses of the original commentaries and generating a massive body of Dante studies, available in journals and books. Ideally, the useful information and the good scholarship would make their way into the commentaries accompanying the text and benefit all readers. But this has not been the case, for commentaries tend to be either neglectful or unimaginative, privileging a fraction of available sources and sometimes simply drawing on previous commentaries. In short, the *Divine Comedy* has generated a massive amount of scholarship, but due to its very massiveness and its uneven quality, we do not have a convenient way of sorting it out and making the best information about the poem's background easily available.

While any correct information we gain is ideally valuable to us, interpretations may be ignorant or prejudiced or simply funny, or they may be enlightening or even incontrovertible. Different trends tend to develop in different historical periods. We have inherited, as part of our traditional interpretation, certain assumptions developed in the romantic and postromantic periods that have, however, been challenged by an important school of American criticism that I will discuss later. A standard conservative twentieth-century view of Dante represents him as politically motivated and interprets the poem as having a literal dramatic level that stands for an abstract theological or sometimes political level. Such a view is generally sympathetic to the politics it discovers in the poem and is dismissive of, or even hostile to, the theology. Implicit in traditional presentations of Dante is the distinction between his allegory, or the abstract doctrine he represents as the "other meaning," and his message of political passion and moral indignation. This distinction is neither consciously expressed in those works in which it is implied, nor is it valid, but it is helpful in clarifying some of the problems we find in conservative readings of the *Divine Comedy*. Let us deal first with common conservative attitudes regarding allegory.

Until recently, no radical change had occurred in the typical understanding of how Dante's allegory works. From the beginning it had generally been taken for granted that Dante said one thing but meant another. His allegory was therefore like a puzzle whose message could be worked out from the clues provided by the literal level. The assumption was that there was an easily formulated abstract meaning that was the solution or interpretation of the allegory. While arguments over the particular solutions continued sometimes through many generations, it was not questioned that the literal level dramatized points of abstract doctrine. The romantics, however, while accepting that this was the nature of Dante's allegory as he intended it, felt a distinct distaste for its lack of spontaneity, which they expressed by disregarding the allegory and focusing their attention on the drama to be found in the literal level. Along with what they thought to be the allegory, they often dismissed the theology found in the poem, or better, they dismissed both, assuming them to be the same. Heroic readings of characters in Hell flourished along with the suggestion that even Dante did not deeply believe the doctrines that dictated some facets of his representation. Francesca, Farinata, and Ulysses, for instance, were in Hell because of beliefs Dante's age forced on him; but deep inside himself, he admired and sympathized with them.

Early in the twentieth century Benedetto Croce formulated a theory that rejected Dante's allegory on aesthetic grounds. Allegory, being doctrinal and artificial, was not intuitive expression and therefore not poetry. While Croce did not deny Dante's poetic value, he considered him to be at his best when his instinct overruled his intention so that, despite himself, his passion burst through his rigid doctrine. Croce's criticism gave theoretical legitimacy to the aversion for theology that had been felt by the romantics and by all of those who in different ways attempted to isolate Dante from his religious beliefs. While the suggestion that so venerable a poet was in any way unpoetic was too extreme for the Italian critics to accept wholeheartedly, moderate forms of Croce's teaching influenced the next generation of Italians and they continue to be detectable in traditional readings of the poem, even in readings by non-Italians.

While the generations before us assumed an equivalency between allegory and doctrine in Dante, they also attributed another, nonallegorical message to his poem. Dante's poem, we often hear, was the result of his political bitterness, his opposition to the pope, or even to the Church itself. It was his way of attacking his enemies with words, of voicing his frustration, or even of gaining enough recognition to force his city to invite him back. We may hear the *Divine Comedy* described as the poetic statement of a Guelf turned Ghibelline, of the first Italian patriot, or even of a Protestant before the fact. It is true that Dante suffered as an exile, it is true that Dante saw Pope Boniface as a great villain, and it is true that Dante was an imperialist. It is not true, however, that he was a supporter of the Ghibellines, and it is not true that he opposed the Church as an institution. It is not necessary to guess at Dante's political opinions, for he voices them very clearly in the *Divine Comedy*. But these opinions are only a secondary part of the vision that he represents as happening in the other world because it extends beyond the limitations of this world; and they are certainly not his "other meaning."

To summarize, traditional readings of the *Divine Comedy* such as we find in the typical commentaries accompanying a text or translation, separate the dramatic literal level from the abstract theological level and, at the same time, they also seem to dismiss the theology they take to be the intended meaning in favor of a secular message they arbitrarily attribute to the poem, sometimes in defiance of what the poem plainly says. These are the worst faults of such readings: obvious facts about the poem, which is deeply Christian in its intention and its mood, are disregarded; there is no unity between the poetry and its meaning; the poem is not interpreted as a whole but piece by piece as if it were a collection of statements or an anthology of episodes. These problems have been answered in recent years by two American critics, Charles Singleton and John Freccero, who have revolutionized our approach to Dante. Despite some protest, mostly from extreme conservatives unwilling to let go of assumptions held for so long, they have convinced the rest of the world of Dante studies that there is a better way.

The radical change that Charles Singleton brought about was based on a premise that was so simple and direct as to be virtually irrefutable: Dante wrote a medieval poem that is best interpreted through an understanding of the deeply Christian medieval way of thinking. With dramatic results, he appealed to us to lay aside our modern and secular prejudices and to examine the poem as Dante might have conceived it. He convinced us that by disregarding theology as uninteresting to us, we were not only misunderstanding Dante's allegory, but his poetics as well. In John Freccero's words, ". . . it is the unique and permanent contribution of Charles Singleton to have brought poetics and thematics together in the interpretation of the poem. By refusing to accept the traditional dichotomy between poetry and belief, . . . he demonstrated the relevance of theology not only to the literary archeologist, but also to the literary critic."[1]

Singleton's study of Dante stressed obvious, and yet often ignored or disregarded, facts about the poem, such as the distinction between Dante the character in the poem, who has not yet been through the experience narrated, and Dante the poet, who is recalling the experience by which he was so transformed; or the relevance of Saint Augustine's literary rendering of his conversion to Dante's story of his journey to God through sin and its rejection. But Singleton is best known for using Dante's own words to overturn age-old assumptions about Dante's allegory. The allegory of the *Divine Comedy,* Singleton submitted, is to be understood as analogous to the divine allegory the poet and his age saw in Scripture and in nature. Different from man-made allegories, God's is written into reality. If Singleton is right that Dante's allegory is modelled on God's, then we no longer have to choose between rejecting it as unpoetic or accepting it as extraneous doctrine, because in such an allegory the source of truth is reality itself or, in the case of the poem, the literal level. In other words, we are no longer asked to discover what Dante means instead of what he says, but rather to search for the significance *of* what he says *in* what he says. His is not, as Singleton put it, an allegory of "this for that," but one of "this and that." Such an allegory, although theological, does not point to abstract doctrine nor does it have a disposable literal level, any more than Creation or the Bible or history do. The relation of the poem's literal level to its allegory is analogous to that of reality to its meaning and, in some sense, the literal level, as the dramatization of Dante's spiritual experience, is indeed real.

Of course, Singleton alone did not change our view; he profited from other studies of Dante—especially noteworthy are those of Erich Auerbach—and from improved studies of the Middle Ages, a period that was beginning to be re-evaluated after generations of comparative neglect. But Singleton's influence and importance cannot be over-stated, nor can he be praised too highly for refusing—so different from others—to let the prejudices of his day cloud his reading.

Although his success was due to his refusal to accept handed-down assumptions, Singleton did hold the one important assumption that the poem is coherent. This assumption is also at the heart of John Freccero's art as a critic. Freccero approaches Dante's text with the unrelenting belief that there is a reason for everything in it, that it is finally intelligible. By reconstructing the background on which a line or a *terzina* might have been composed, he not only enlightens the passage in question but the rest of the poem as well; for now we see how the passage fits the rest, how it plays a part in the whole. Single-ton taught us to open our minds to the subtlety of the theological background we had so disregarded and treated so superficially; he taught us not to underestimate Saint Augustine's influence on Dante; and he taught us to be more attentive to the text itself. Freccero better than anyone else developed those lessons in his criticism, not only showing us meanings we had ignored but showing us dimensions we had ignored, leading us not to answers but to new questions and with them a new sense of the depth of Dante's poem and of the rewards of the interpretive search that Dante has inspired for so long.

The influence of Singleton and Freccero has dominated modern Dante criticism in America for a generation and has become influential in Italy more recently. But the direction they have given to Dante stud-ies is not a temporary one, for they have broadened and deepened the field, not narrowed it. Endowed with superior ability and inspired by respect for the text, they have simply shown us how to do better what we wanted to do all along: interpret the words Dante wrote in our unending search for the "other meaning."

The reading I will give in the following pages will echo through-out with Freccero's and Singleton's lessons. In these brief chapters I will try to present to the reader some of the dynamics of the text as I see them. But I see them as I have learned to see them from others, especially from Freccero and Singleton, from whom I borrow too often to acknowledge them each time. I will strive to offer, even if only in general terms, interpretations of important facets of the poem so closely based on the text itself as to be, although modern, as nearly incontrovertible as possible. Although I will find it necessary at times to generalize and to move back and forth over the text, I will try to avoid descriptive introductory remarks available in any commentary and to move through the poem following its natural development.

A READING

CHAPTER IV

The *Inferno*

INTRODUCTION AND STRUCTURE

Beatrice. The *Divine Comedy* is Dante's story of how he was guided through the decreasing circles of Hell to the center of the earth and the bottom of the universe; then through a tunnel to the surface of the opposite Southern Hemisphere and up the great mountain of Purgatory to the Garden of Eden on its top; and, finally, through the nine spheres of the heavens to the end of space and beyond, into the spiritual dimension of the Empyrean or the Kingdom of God. The poem is universal in the literal sense of the word, for it portrays the universe and explores its meaning. But Dante's journey through the universe, the realm of experience of all his readers, is also his journey to the particular woman he loved and to his personal salvation.

Although Dante's literary works contain almost no information about him in the ordinary sense, they comprise an amazingly exhaustive spiritual autobiography, an account of what he perceived to be the meaning of his life or the message of universal value contained in his particular experience. Dante's story is neither one of sequential events and facts, nor one of his meditations and ideas, but rather the story of the development in his soul of a compelling vision that demanded expression. His whole life, as he recounts it, was focused on a woman, Beatrice, who entered it early, who died young, and whom he never forgot. He tells us that she was beautiful but not what she looked like;

he tells us that she was virtuous but not what her particular actions, skills, or tastes were; he tells us that she died but not how; and he chooses not to tell us that she was married. Dante not only suppresses external details about Beatrice but alters facts as well, for virtually everything about her life on Earth is incidental and secondary to the message she brought—to her significance.

Dante's account of the early years of his love is to be found in his youthful work, the *Vita Nuova*. According to the *Vita Nuova*, Dante met Beatrice—whose name means "she who makes blessed" or "she who leads to salvation"—when he was nine years old, and that meeting marked the beginning of his spiritual life. He was to meet her again with some frequency throughout his youth and, while these meetings consisted of no more than a polite exchange of greetings, the complexity of his reaction to them was inversely proportionate to their content. The consequences of being greeted by Beatrice—the related Italian words "*saluto*" and "*salute*" mean, respectively, "greeting" and "salvation"—or even just seeing her at a distance, included trembling, blanching, fainting, becoming feverish, and losing weight. Days of agonized dwelling on each brief encounter produced the poems that form the basis of the *Vita Nuova*.

The *Vita Nuova* tells of two critical turning points in the story. The first is when Beatrice, concerned about gossip, discontinues her greeting of him. On the one hand, the loss is tremendous, for her greeting was all he had of her and all he asked for. But, on the other hand, it brings him to the realization that even more precious than these brief encounters is his love for her and that his very raison d'être is to praise her and express her great worthiness. This, he decides, cannot be taken away from him by anyone. But the security this realization brings is shattered by the next and most important crisis, Beatrice's death. However passively, Beatrice had been present as the real person constituting the object of his passionate love and the recipient of his devout praise. She has now left the earth and has been effectively taken away from him. Her death brings on a period of grief and confusion during which a kind and loving woman comforts Dante but also causes in him a severe state of internal conflict. To love anyone except

Beatrice seems to be a betrayal of her and of himself but, at the same time, to refuse all love now that she is gone seems to be a renunciation of love itself, to which his life has long been committed. The *Vita Nuova* ends almost abruptly with a sonnet representing his heart reaching toward Heaven for Beatrice, followed by the famous closing words:

> After this sonnet there appeared to me a marvellous vision in which I saw things which made me decide to write no more of this blessed one until I could do so more worthily. And to this end I apply myself as much as I can, as she indeed knows. Thus, if it shall please Him by whom all things live that my life continue for a few years, I hope to compose concerning her what has never been written in rhyme of any woman. And then may it please Him who is Lord of courtesy that my soul may go to see the glory of my lady, that is of the blessed Beatrice, who now in glory beholds the face of Him *qui est per omnia secula benedictus.*[2]

The *Vita Nuova,* here described only in schematic terms, is the best introduction to Dante's masterpiece, for it presents the poet's own choice of what we need to know about him, and expresses the hope that he will write what was to become the *Divine Comedy.* Years passed between that expression of hope and its fulfillment but, as promised, those years were dedicated to preparation and study. The Dante we read in the *Divine Comedy* has developed intellectually almost beyond recognition and is now in possession of the greatest degree of knowledge available to his age. But the tormented autobiographical character we find in the dark wood is still, above all, Beatrice's lover.

The Dark Wood and The Hill. The opening lines of the *Divine Comedy,* describing the poet's struggle to find his way out of a dark wood and back to the light of the sun, presuppose that "our life" is, at least metaphorically, a journey to a determined goal, that is to say, a journey that can have a right or a wrong road. Dante's principal symbol is also established early: the sun, "the planet that leads man

straight on every road," (1.17–18) or the force without which the journey of life cannot be successful. To lose the sun is to lose the way,
which is so tragic that "death is hardly more" (1.7). Given these uni-
versals, we find our character lost on the road of his particular life.
Sometime between Beatrice's death and this moment, her lover has
ended up in a dark and frightening wood. Perhaps he has been there
ever since her death. In any case, he is now struggling to escape and
is comforted by the upward form of a hill bathed in the light of the
sun. The sunlit hill holds out to him the hope of finding again his lost
way.

The landscape in the prologue scene is clearly symbolic and psy-
chological; Dante expresses with it the state of his soul, not the literal
place of any period in his life. It matters little that he speaks alternately
of a dark wood, or of a valley, or of a sea in which one might be
drowning, or of a lake in his heart, for all of these are images of an
internal experience. And it is his soul, "*l'animo mio*" (1.25) that is
running from the terrible night of this experience and looking back at
the pass "which never yet let any go alive" (1.27). And yet, as Charles
Singleton points out, suddenly at line 28 a body tired from running
away is introduced, not as a metaphor but as a literal presence that
will be with us for the rest of the poem: "I rested my wearied body
for a little."

We usually call this body the "pilgrim," meaning Dante's former
self as the character of his poem, and we distinguish him from the
poet who is now writing from the point of view gained by the experience he recalls. This character seems to enter the poem as a literal
presence, physically worn out by the spiritual anguish of escaping
from a metaphorical wood of distress. He rests a little and then begins
to walk up a hill that, different from the wood, seems really to be
there, but at the same time seems to stand for something other than
itself, the hope of the sun at its top. In other words, the pilgrim literally
walks toward his goal but along a path of abstractions. This attempt
fails because of three allegorical beasts who block his way and drive
him back to "where the sun is silent" (1.60). The meaning of the hill
and the beasts on it becomes retrospectively clearer as we read the rest

of the poem. What is immediately clear is that the pilgrim's attempt at recovery through ascent only precipitates him back to what is now simply called "the place below" (1.61). Were it not for the help that arrives at this critical moment, the story would end tragically here.

But, as the pilgrim loses the "hope of the ascent" (1.54), pushed back by a "she wolf," a shadowy figure emerges from the desolation of what is now called "the great waste" (1.64). In his terror and despair, the pilgrim begs this apparition for help. The one who "seemed weak from long silence" (1.63) identifies himself in nine lines that with shocking clarity reveal him to be Virgil, the great poet of the Roman Empire, idealized and loved by Dante beyond any other. The better we know Virgil's poetry and understand Dante's reading of it, the more we can appreciate the drama of the pilgrim's realization that he is facing the miraculous real presence of this awesome figure. "Not man; once I was man" (1.67). The voice of the ancient spirit comes to life here on the hill, somewhat reminiscent of how the pilgrim's body appeared earlier in the prologue, and offers to lead him to his goal by "another road" (1.91). After an initial impulse to follow the "famous sage" (1.89) wherever he leads, the pilgrim, realizing that the journey is to be to the world of the dead, has second thoughts. But his doubts are dispelled when Virgil tells him that his miraculous appearance is the result of Beatrice's intervention. As the pilgrim retreated in panic down the hill, the Virgin Mary saw him and called Saint Lucy who in turn called Beatrice to show her the terrible danger threatening her lover. Beatrice's instant response was to descend from Heaven and summon Virgil to guide the pilgrim off the hill. The pilgrim's lifelong love for Beatrice has been rewarded by her intervention at his moment of greatest peril. Once he descends from the allegorical hill of abstractions to follow Virgil on a path to Beatrice, the concretely defined and fictionally real voyage begins and its message unfolds. Part of that message has its roots in these very early cantos and in the role they assign to Virgil.

Virgil. Virgil, who lived in the first century B.C. and witnessed the birth of the Roman Empire under Caesar Augustus, was the greatest of the Latin poets. His masterpiece is the *Aeneid,* a national epic that he was commissioned to write as a celebration of the new Empire. It tells the story of the Trojan Aeneas who, guided by his mother Venus, escaped burning Troy and set out to accomplish a mission. This mission, whose success was decreed by Jupiter himself, was to lead the surviving Trojans to Italy to form a new race. Like Ulysses' voyage, Aeneas's is long and fraught with hardship and suffering, not the least of which is the loss along the way of Anchises, his father and chief source of encouragement and advice. However, in book 6, he is granted a visit to the underworld where he is able to talk to his father's shade and to learn from him the far-reaching purpose of his mission. By revealing the future, Anchises is able to show Aeneas that the great burden he endures is to a still greater end, that of generating a race of unprecedented virtue and unlimited power. His descendents will be the Romans, who will govern the world with strength, order, and mercy.

Virgil's celebration of the Roman Empire and the Augustan age is carried even further by Dante who, already in *Inferno* 2, speaks of Virgil's hero as chosen by God

> to be father of glorious Rome and of
> her Empire, and both of these were
> established—if we would speak
> rightly of them—to be the holy
> place where sits the successor of
> the great Peter.
>
> (2.20–24)

In Dante's reading, beyond what Virgil could possibly have known, Rome's glory was secondary to its role in preparing the world for the birth of Christ and establishing Rome as the providentially chosen center of the Church. And so Virgil, who was born under "the good Augustus," but also under "the false and lying gods," witnessed and testified to the birth of the Roman Empire, having no way of knowing that what he represented as an accomplished glory was only a preparation for a far greater event. Dante's paradoxical reading of Virgil is at one and the same time distorting, in that he connects the *Aeneid* to a message unknown to its author, and remarkably loyal to its authority, even to the point of assigning credibility and historical truth to Virgil's legends and literary inventions.

But the *Aeneid* and Dante's reading of it are both far more complex than the imperialism expressed by Virgil and reinterpreted by Dante. Virgil's triumphalism represents only one side of his poem. It is the side that reflects the political optimism of the great Augustan era and the Stoic philosophy that guided the thought of his day. Roman stoicism preached principles of collective good, of civic duties, of virtue as its own reward, and of the sacrifice of individual goals to social and political ones. But stoicism promised nothing to the individual, whose choice was either to submit willingly to a cosmic order or to submit unwillingly. Aeneas, the long-suffering father of the Romans, is certainly a Stoic hero, from whom the gods demand again and again that he put aside his personal happiness in view of his mission and that he endure pain, suffering, hardship, and grief along his fated path.

At the same time, although Virgil is perhaps Stoic enough to believe in the inevitability of personal tragedy, he does not willingly accept it. He recognizes and celebrates a great deal of collective and cosmic good but throughout his poem he rejects in frustration and grief the suffering his characters must endure. Numerous victims fall along the way of Aeneas's journey and populate poignantly the *Aeneid*. Dido, Aeneas's lover who is manipulated and destroyed by the gods protecting the great voyage, is the most famous victim of the onslaught of the Roman destiny. But many others are unforgiveably destroyed along Aeneas's path: Euryalus, Nisus, Turnus, Camilla, and Pallas. These are all young and brave warriors whose very youth and vulnerability lead them both bravely and foolishly into danger, and whose loss the poet mourns unconsoled. They, and others like them, fighting on Aeneas's side or against him, are as much Virgil's heroes as Aeneas and Anchises are. But, unlike the pains of the protagonist and his father, their suffering, in Virgil's eyes, is not linked to the glory of Rome; it is gratuitous, cruel, and unacceptable. This is the dark side of the *Aeneid*, without which it would not be the great poem it is. It seems excessive to say that, because of this side of Virgil's vision, his praise of Rome is insincere. Certainly Dante did not read the poem as subversive in any way. But Virgil's vision is tormented, full of unanswered questions, and ultimately tragic, for nothing he sees in the order of the cosmos or of the state mitigates the suffering and futility that can afflict the life of an individual. Dante did not miss the point of the pathos that is so much a part of the *Aeneid*, but he did see in Christianity the resolution of Virgil's unanswerable questions.

As Virgil invites the pilgrim down off the hill, he announces the coming of the enigmatic Greyhound who will save the world from the seemingly undefeatable she wolf. Whatever the Greyhound and the she wolf stand for, Virgil's prophecy is an announcement not just of order but of the triumph of good, of the deliverance of man from a seemingly undefeatable evil. The providence implied by Virgil's words, different from that of the *Aeneid*, encompasses all things in its "wisdom and love and valour" (1.104).

> He shall be salvation to that low-
> lying Italy for which the virgin
> Camilla and Euryalus and Turnus and
> Nisus died of their wounds.
>
> (1.106–8)

Readers of the *Aeneid* will recognize in the names remembered by Virgil four of its most moving examples of the senseless violation of youth by death and might well be shocked to see the fatal wounds of Camilla, Euryalus, Turnus, and Nisus transformed from those of victims to those of martyrs. To understand Virgil as a character in the *Divine Comedy,* we must understand that Dante created him from his reading of the *Aeneid,* but also transformed him into what he might have been if he had been reawakened form the dead and made aware of Christianity. Like us, Dante saw in the *Aeneid* an irresolvable conflict between political and cosmic order on the one hand and individual tragedy on the other. But that he also believed that Christ had brought the answer to Virgil's hopelessness is an essential part of his re-creation of Virgil as the most important and most complex character in the *Divine Comedy.*

The Message on the Gates and The Nature of Sin. Hell's message of divine justice and eternal hopelessness is written on its face, in the famous inscription over the gate with which canto 3 opens:

> THROUGH ME THE WAY INTO THE WOEFUL CITY.
> THROUGH ME THE WAY TO THE ETERNAL PAIN.
> THROUGH ME THE WAY AMONG THE LOST PEOPLE.
> JUSTICE MOVED MY MAKER ON HIGH,
> DIVINE POWER MADE ME AND SUPREME WISDOM
>   AND PRIMAL LOVE;
> BEFORE ME NOTHING WAS CREATED BUT ETERNAL
>   THINGS AND I ENDURE ETERNALLY.
> ABANDON EVERY HOPE, YE THAT ENTER.   (3.1–9)

The inscription is like a label, ominously pointing to what is behind it, the eternal pain and suffering that divine justice demands from the unjust. The sign on Hell's gate allows for no constructive experience within, but it is also a sign whose meaning is clearly as urgent as the desctructive consequences of not knowing or not fearing God are irreversible. Besides damnation, interpretation and understanding lie behind the terrible inscription and, in Dante's story, the pilgrim's unique immunity to the one is granted so that he may acquire the others. Like us, he enters Hell as a reader of its message, as one for whom the words alone, clear as they may be, are not a sufficient deterrent. The pilgrim's literal passing beyond the words written on the gate is the first step in his journey to the experience and understanding of their message.

Hell, as its gate states, is a place made by God, specifically by the Trinitarian God of power, wisdom, and love. But the suffering and eternal pain of the lost souls within are of their own making. The justice that made Hell is reflected in the order that the Creator of all things imposes upon the world of the damned so that, despite the meaninglessness of their suffering, they inevitably express the real guilt of denying the source of all good. The various punishments of the damned turn out to be concrete versions of their choices in life, not just arbitrary consequences of their sins, but semantically tied to them. The storm that blows the souls who were ruled by their passions around and about, exemplifies their failure to control their desires. The tombs that confine the heretics eternally are monuments to their denial of the idea of life after death. The word Dante uses for the significant relation of the soul's torment to its guilt is "*contrapasso*," which guarantees the survival of justice even among its enemies who, ironically, express its principles while eternally suffering the consequences of their own unjust lives. A further dimension of Hell's irony comes from the fact that its message, governed by order and justice, has no audience, for its prisoners cannot read it. There is no audience, that is, except the pilgrim, whose unique visit is the subjecct of the *Inferno*.

The story begins when Virgil, sent by Beatrice, sent by Saint Lucy, sent by the mother of God, takes the pilgrim by the hand and leads him into "*le segrete cose*," "the things that are hidden" (3.21). The pilgrim travels among the damned souls, hears the sad truths of their earthly lives as only God knew them, and consequently discovers secrets and dangers in his own soul. As he descends deeper and deeper into this underground of God's creation, things more deeply hidden are revealed to him. Beneath anything that can be seen by other men, the human soul is either damned or saved and, each time, human nature is perverted or redeemed. The hidden things of Hell are revealed to the pilgrim so that he will gain understanding of his human self; he, not the souls he encounters, is the protagonist.

These considerations can, I believe, help us avoid two of the most common misconceptions about Dante's work: that he has mixed feelings about the damnation of some of the souls in Hell and that the *Inferno* provides him with a platform from which to express disapproval of personages of his day by performing a kind of literary damnation on them. The first of these misconceptions comes from failing to recognize the role of the pilgrim as the main character of the poem and confusing his often tormented response to what and whom he discovers in Hell with the authorial voice of the poet presenting this fiction as the story of his former self and his former responses. The second misconception is primarily the result of the reader's failure to recognize the most important of Dante's premises: that God, not he, made Hell. While ultimately the *Inferno* does, of course, represent Dante's work, its message depends on the fiction that is written on the gates: "JUSTICE MOVED MY MAKER ON HIGH, / DIVINE POWER MADE ME AND SUPREME WISDOM AND PRIMAL LOVE" (3.3–5).

Each soul reveals things about itself to the pilgrim and simultaneously things about the pilgrim to himself, but, as I suggested earlier, it also plays a part in the larger message that, unfolding over all of Hell, presents sin as degeneration and corruption, and the perversion of human nature as the essence of its guilt. Dante's Infernal theology, in fact, revolves around the understanding of human nature as good and of sin as its perversion. While all of man's natural desire is for good, because of Adam's Fall the will's perversion toward evil is possible. Hell is divided into nine circles belonging to three main categories and further subdivided by variations enclosed in each circle, but its overall plan presents a descending progression toward ever increasing guilt or corruption of the will. In order to read the *Inferno* properly, it is necessary to have an unequivocal understanding that sin is an act of the will. In other words, it is committed knowingly and intentionally. Many oversimplified or wrongheaded readings of the *Inferno* stem from incomprehension of this premise, possibly because even if the premise is simple it nevertheless requires speculation on the extremely complex subject of human nature.

The questions Dante is asking are not about what is right and what is wrong; they are about how we constantly embrace what we know to be wrong. Socrates thought it so unreasonable that a person would choose bad over good that he attributed such choices to ignorance. A man who chooses to do wrong must necessarily have failed to realize truly that what he did was wrong, otherwise his action would be impossible. A helpful way for modern readers to think of the problem might be through an example relating to health rather than morality, to which we are less sensitive than the Middle Ages were. Suppose someone is on a diet because he wants to lose weight and to improve his life at many levels and therefore to become happier. But, attracted to fattening food, he trades his hope of happiness for the immediate gratifaction of eating. If this action seems unreasonable, we should try to imagine how much more incomprehensible it might be to trade eternal beatitude for a moment's pleasure, or for anything else. Sin is treated by Dante as irrational, mysterious, and as complicated as human nature itself. But its definition is simple; it is a knowing and willing choice of wrong over right.

It is important for Dante's readers to understand that none of his sinners is innocent ("By this way no good spirit ever passes" [3.127]), but it is equally important to understand that their sins themselves are not ultimately the reason they are condemned to Hell, which is rather that, having sinned, they failed to repent. In Dante's faith, a soul can only be saved by turning to God for forgiveness. A mere sin of weakness can damn one who does not recognize his weakness and ask God for strength, while the greatest act of malice will be forgiven if divine mercy is invoked. A sinner, therefore, in Dante's Hell is one who, having willfully committed actions he knew to be wrong, failed to repent. While there are no exceptions to the last part of this definition—that is, no soul in Hell turned to God for salvation—Hell begins with two groups that do not correspond to the first part, the neutrals and the inhabitants of Limbo; the first did not sin willfully and the second did not sin knowingly. Still, in radically different ways they illustrate the basic principles that underlie Dante's representation of human failure.

The Structure of Hell. The neutrals, who are kept on this side of the river Acheron and outside of Hell proper, are described as never having been alive and as unworthy even of Hell. Their unique position serves to stress the importance of the will in damnation. Human life is conceived by Christianity as powerfully dramatic. The soul is given freedom along with life and the choices it makes in this life will determine whether it will live in the next one in everlasting fulfillment or in everlasting pain. To remain neutral or noncommittal is to stand back from the drama of choosing God or choosing against Him and, by rejecting freedom, to reject the gift of life itself.

The souls in Limbo are in every way the opposite of the neutrals. They are unbaptized babies and people born before the coming of Christ. These neither refused to choose nor chose evil but, because they did not know Christ, they could not choose Him and be saved through Him. Excluded from salvation but not punished, they are mysteriously suspended between good and evil in "a blaze of light which was enclosed in a hemisphere of darkness" (4.68–69). Virgil is one of these souls. Leaving Limbo, he and the pilgrim enter the part of the universe "where no light shines" (4.151). The illumination in Limbo is not celestial, it does not come from the sun or the other stars, rather it is the earthly light of fire. Nevertheless it marks symbolically the radical difference between the innocent inhabitants of Limbo and the guilty souls below them.

The main structure of Hell begins after Limbo with circles devoted to those who lost their souls through incontinence, or weakness. The natural inclinations followed by these souls were not in themselves evil but should have been controlled because they could cause evil. The sins in the early cantos are sins of appetite, immoral actions committed because the will gave in to the desire for a lesser good to the sacrifice of a greater one and, ultimately, traded everlasting fulfilment of all desires for the satisfaction of a momentary passion. The desire for evil is no more the cause of the actions of the incontinent than to become fat is the reason a dieter eats fattening food, but in both cases the main goal may be lost to the weakness of momentarily disregarding it.

The great difference between these sinners and those found lower in Hell is marked concretely by the walls of Dis. Within Dis, another name for the city of Hell, are punished the violent and the fraudulent. Violence and fraud are subdivisions of malice, which includes all sins committed with the intent of doing evil. The will of the souls within the walls of Dis was corrupted to the point that their purpose was to do what was wrong, not necessarily because it was wrong but, at least, despite its wrongness. If a man strikes another man because he has lost his temper, the goal of his action may be to vent his anger, not to harm the other. But if his goal is to harm the other, his sin is not one of passion, but of malice. The more calculated the malice, the greater the corruption and degree of sin. Hence the further division between sins of violence and sins of fraud.

The first-time reader of the *Divine Comedy* need not trouble himself with all the categories of sin and the problems related to their interpretation, but he should keep in mind one all-important principle: the descent into Hell moves toward ever-increasing corruption of human nature. A sin of weakness, or giving in to a natural passion, is the first step toward generating unnatural passions, or the desire for evil. When passion passes, the will to sin passes with it, while malice becomes a habit, replacing the natural desire for good with a corrupted will that accepts and even approves the evil implicit in its actions. Despite this difference, the surrender to weakness can be the beginning of true corruption, for when the will turns away from God, albeit momentarily, it also starts to take a distorted view of its action, to rationalize or to justify what it would have condemned before it was tempted. The seeds of corruption are to be found even in sins of weakness. Still, because these sins come from natural inclinations, they are divided by the great wall of Dis from the malice produced against nature by the corrupted will.

To return to the pilgrim's voyage, it is at this wall that the most serious crisis of the infernal voyage occurs. The devils and the Furies band together to stop the pilgrim and his guide from entering their city. Virgil tries to exert the authority that God has given him for this mission to subdue them, but they ignore him and threaten to bring out the Gorgon Medusa, the sight of whom turns men to stone. Virgil covers the pilgrim's eyes with his own hands to protect him and anxiously awaits help, which comes in the form of a "heavenly messenger," perhaps an angel, against whom the devils and mythological creatures are helpless. They retreat and allow passage to the two travellers. This episode presents many interpretive difficulties, but it is clearly an important and critical point in the structure of the voyage, a juncture at which additional grace or help from God is required. The poet demands that we ask what this crisis is, and what new fortitude the pilgrim needs before entering these walls.

There is a similar crisis in the prologue scene. The pilgrim looks up to the sun and sets out on a path toward it, but the path is impeded by three symbolic beasts, a leopard, a lion, and a she wolf. The *Divine Comedy* is not usually allegorical in the way that these two episodes are, that is in the sense that its representations do not mean themselves but something else. The allegory of the *Divine Comedy* is better described as having both a literal meaning and another meaning, than as having another meaning instead of a literal meaning. But the scene on the hill and the scene at the walls of Dis are not typical of the *Comedy* in this sense. We are confronted by strange representations that cannot be understood literally. In both scenes the pilgrim seems very near failure. In both scenes help is sent from above and tragedy is avoided. One of the most common interpretations of the three beasts—despite the not-insurmountable problems it presents—is that they represent the three general categories of sin that are punished in Hell: incontinence, violence, and fraud. Sin, therefore, impedes the pilgrim's journey toward the sun. If this is so, then the leopard, the first beast, represents fraud, the lion violence, and the she wolf with her insatiable appetite incontinence. With some difficulty, the pilgrim makes his way past the first two beasts but is almost driven back to the dark wood by the third. Indeed, he would be driven back, if Virgil were not called in by Beatrice to bring help from Heaven as the only way past the terrible danger. Because of the fierce beast and the danger she presents, Virgil informs the pilgrim that he must take a different voyage, a voyage that turns out to be the one through Hell.

That there is a relation between the attempted voyage up the hill and the successful voyage through Hell is clear from Virgil's words and seems to be confirmed by an interpretation of the beasts as corresponding to the categories of sin around which Hell is structured. But why are they reversed in order? Why does the beast who stands for the least grievous type of sin seem to be the most dangerous to the pilgrim? Why is it that the crisis inside Hell occurs just as the pilgrim approaches the domain of malice, represented on the hill by the other two beasts? We must conclude that what is the greatest obstacle on the hill is the least obstacle to his voyage through Hell. And it is this conclusion that leads us to see Dante's purpose far more clearly. The journey on the hill was an outward journey, the journey past the inscription with Virgil is an inward journey, without which the outward one cannot be accomplished. The hill dramatizes the rational approach or, which is the same, the moral approach. The pilgrim chooses the light of the sun over the darkness and danger of the wood. Since the choice is clear, the straight way should be straightforward. But it is not. Whatever interpretation we give to the mysteries of human behavior, Dante would have said that man's tendency to act irrationally was caused by Adam's sin. Because human nature is fallen, it is corruptible. We know what we should do, we know what is good for us, and still we desire and do what is bad for us. Our nature is subject to irrational temptation. But we are not tempted, at least not usually, to do extremely corrupt things; we are tempted to do relatively innocent ones. This, I think, is why it is the wolf, the beast standing for the sins of weakness, who causes the failure of the pilgrim's progress up the hill.

But when the pilgrim enters Hell, when he penetrates the secrets of human nature, of its corruptibility, of his own corruptibility, the situation is reversed. He recognizes a little something of himself, sometimes a lot of himself, in the lost souls. But, while no radical change in his understanding of himself is brought about by his congeniality with the souls who were lost through weakness, only by spiritual trauma can he face himself in the soul of a murderer or a traitor. What is easiest to avoid doing outwardly, is in some sense most difficult to face inwardly. Perhaps, when Virgil covers the pilgrim's eyes to keep him from looking into the face of Medusa who will turn him to stone, he is also forcing him to look inward and face himself.

The pilgrim is horrified by all of the sights of Hell, but upper Hell does not contain the kind of surprises that the city of Dis does. Francesca, Ciacco, Filippo are where he might have expected them to be. Their sins were known to him and outwardly manifested in actions. But within Dis he will find souls of persons he admired, respected, even loved. He will find great men who seemed to have great worth. He will find souls whose sins were known only to God. Dante's purpose in writing the *Inferno* is not to preach about which actions are right and which are wrong, but to dig deeply into the human soul in search of the motivations hidden there, in search of the inner reality of himself as a human being, potentially corruptible beyond recognition as such. The walls of Dis hold secrets that cannot be penetrated without crisis and trauma, and this crisis reflects the reason that earlier, in order for the pilgrim's journey to the sun to be successful, Virgil had to rescue him from the hill and lead him by another way.

One thing remains to be said about the general pattern of Hell and the principles guiding it. Morality, for all its worth, does not lead directly to salvation. Although human nature is basically rational, it is also fallen, spiritually sick and weak, and it cannot recover from the consequences of this state through its own strength. For the fall to be counteracted, in Dante's theology, the soul must humbly seek its strength from Christ, it must recognize its own weakness, and accept Christ as its savior. Morality is the measure of a man's innate or acquired strength but, however great, if he relies on his own strength, he will fail to possess the prime Christian virtue: humility. The journey into Hell is also a journey toward humility. It is different from the one up the hill because it is made with divine help sent in the form of Virgil and repeated through the messenger at the critical walls of Dis. While Hell teaches the pilgrim to turn away from corruption, it also prepares him through humility for the offer of salvation.

GREAT CHARACTERS OF HELL

Francesca. The first soul who the pilgrim speaks with is also possibly the most famous character of the *Inferno*: Francesca da Rimini. The circle is that of "the carnal sinners who submit reason to desire" (5:38–39). Francesca's story of how her brother-in-law Paolo was moved by her beauty and she by his love, how they sat and read together of Lancelot and Guinevere, and finally how they were drawn into each other's arms by proximity, chemistry, and the tale of a great love, has moved centuries of audiences. The couple were murdered by Francesca's husband, Paolo's brother, and are damned to Hell for their adulterous actions. Together in Hell as in their last embrace, their story is immortalized by Dante's poetry. Francesca's words move us to sympathy. We are not presented with a woman whose major concern was sensual gratification, who degraded herself in undiscrimating pursuit of pleasure, but with a woman who gave in to the most natural of all desires, who sought love and comfort and closeness. And, lest we think that Dante does not share our distaste for the choice of her as the first representative of unforgiven human guilt, we do well to recall how he describes his response to her at this stage of his journey:

> "Alas, how many sweet thoughts, how
> great desire, brought them to the
> woeful pass!" Then I turned to them
> again to speak and began:
> "Francesca, thy torments make me
> weep for grief and pity."
>
> (5.112–17)

When the story is told, the pilgrim takes a final glance at Paolo, who is silently weeping, and is so overcome by pity that he loses consciousness. Our reaction, mild compared to that which the poet describes as his own, can neither be unexpected nor undesired by him. But if the reader, receptive only to the beauty of Francesca's natural desires, fails to see the insidious nature of her story, then he shares not only her desires, but her tragic self-deception as well. In fact, influenced by their romantic reading, Paolo's and Francesca's imaginations transformed what they clearly knew to be adultery when they first sat down to read into the inevitable result of an irresistible love. By identifying their feelings with the grand-scale romance of the literary lovers and imagining their own passion exalted beyond the domain of moral judgment, they were able to rationalize their desire as something uncontrollable and their surrender to it as guiltless. While Dante certainly expects us to sympathize with the lovers, this surely does not mean that he hopes we will condone their actions, using their story, and *his* book, as they used the book about Lancelot and Guinevere. He has striven rather to point to the danger in his creation.

Were Francesca's feelings not beautiful, neither the pilgrim nor the reader would be moved by them, but neither would there be danger in them. As it stands, her words are dangerous, not because they are beautiful but because, since they *are* beautiful, it is tempting to see them only as we would like them to be. Let us look at Francesca's most famous lines:

> Love, which is quickly kindled in
> the gentle heart, seized this man
> for the fair form that was taken
> from me, and the manner offends me
> still. Love, which absolves no one
> beloved from loving, seized me so
> strongly with his charm that, as
> thou seest, it does not leave me
> yet. Love brought us to one death.
> Caina waits for him who quenched our
> life.
>
> (5.100–107)

Not only are these lines written in the style of Dante's early and idealistic poetry to Beatrice and therefore particularly seductive to the pilgrim, but the obsessive repetition of the word *amor* manipulates him and us into attention to the sentiment, distracting us from the action.

Furthermore, the lines are structured in such a way as to form almost a logical statement of innocence, superficially reproducing the pattern of a syllogism, or a conclusion inevitably resulting from two premises. The premises Francesca seems to give us are that the gentle heart (the phrase used by Dante in his youthful poems, and by others of his time, to denote spiritual nobility and sensitivity to love) is naturally attracted to beauty, and that love demands reciprocation. The rationale for her innocence is powerfully prepared by these premises: Paolo is sensitive and cannot help loving her for her beauty and she cannot help loving him for his love. But, when the conclusion comes, it is not justification but tragedy: "Love brought us to one death." Francesca's tone then takes a dramatic turn with her bitter last line: "Caina waits for him who quenched our life." As she evokes the punishment, greater than hers, that awaits her husband, she also reveals her famous words on love as ultimately charged with violence, revenge, and hatred. As a matter of fact, in these few lines she has already mentioned the murder and her bitterness, but her tone is so lulling that their brutal reality has been obscured. She has also described Paolo's attraction as being for her body (*"la bella persona,"* "the fair form") and her response to him as pleasure (*"piacere"*; here translated "charm"), but the powerful positioning of the word *"amor"* at the beginning of each section and the soft sounds and rhythm of her words keep these details from our attention. These famous lines, beautiful as they are, are ultimately most impressive for the art with which they disguise carnality and violence as innocence and purity.

If we are reluctant to accept a full reading of Francesca, we are not alone, for so is the pilgrim, even as he hears her speak in the context of the howlings and wailings of Hell. He bows his head so long that Virgil becomes preoccupied and at the end, as I have mentioned, the pilgrim even faints from pity. But canto 6 opens with the description of the pilgrim's fainting as the closing of his mind before the sadness of the two, and it points to something more than compassion, the painful experience of recognizing what he did not want to see.

Farinata and Cavalcante. Just inside the walls of Dis, Virgil and the pilgrim come upon a cemetery of open tombs. All around are flames and red-hot tombs from which wailings come forth. Virgil explains to the pilgrim that here are buried the souls of the many and various heretics, who burn more or less according to the gravity of the heresy they embraced. They are arranged by groups corresponding to their misbeliefs. The general division of Hell is discussed by Virgil immediately after the encounter with the heretics and does not include them in the three main categories, no doubt because their guilt does not come from what they did but from what they believed. In any case, the travelers' encounter with the heretics, typical of the *Inferno,* has little to do with heresy in the narrow sense, that is with the refusal to embrace one or more of the Church's central teachings. The souls in the group they approach are referred to as followers of Epicurus "who make the soul die with the body" (10.15). Epicurus, a Greek philosopher, not a heretic, strongly opposed all belief in the afterlife as detrimental to the quality of this life. To believe that the soul dies with the body represents not just a disagreement with a point of doctrine, but a disagreement with religion itself, an intellectual rejection of God. The souls Dante calls followers of Epicurus are nonbelievers and, in retribution for their intellectual position, they are eternally condemned to the tomb, where they believed life would end.

Different from other sinners in Hell, the Epicureans were not morally corrupt, because their choice was an intellectual not a moral one. This becomes especially evident in Farinata degli Uberti, the fierce Ghibelline leader, hated by the Florentines but also responsible for their city's survival. In fact, the Ghibelline Farinata had been the principal force behind the most bloody battle in Florentine memory, the battle of Montaperti between the Guelfs who held power in the city and the Ghibellines who had been exiled by them. The great bloodshed of Montaperti in 1260 was still alive in the unforgiving minds of the Florentines in Dante's time. But to him, Farinata's great victory came after the battle. When the Ghibelline leaders met to discuss the fate of the defeated city and decided that as punishment it should be destroyed, Farinata stood alone against the others and vowed that such action would not be taken "so long as there was life in his body." The other leaders backed off, knowing the strength of this great man. There is no doubt about Dante's admiration for him as a hero of the greatest political virtue, the placing of country over party.

In the tomb next to Farinata's is the soul of another nonbeliever, Cavalcante Cavalcanti, the father of Dante's fellow poet and best friend Guido. As the pilgrim converses with Farinata about their common city, this soul peeks out of his tomb to inquire about Guido and, misunderstanding the pilgrim's reply to mean that his son is dead, drops back down in despair. Farinata, who seems oblivious not only to Cavalcante's interruption and painful misunderstanding, but to his own infernal surroundings as well, continues his conversation about Florence as if nothing at all had happened.

The tall and noble figure of Farinata seems to dominate with his unbending strength the environment around him, commanding respect even from Virgil. Cavalcante, in sharp contrast to him, is an emotional and vulnerable figure, inspiring pity and causing personal sorrow and regret to the pilgrim. The poetic effectiveness of the contrast of the two is often pointed out, the one seeming even larger and more immovable beside the subdued and confused grief of the other. But perhaps more unites the two than distinguishes them. Neither Farinata nor Cavalcante exhibits the kind of moral degeneracy we might expect to find in Dis. On the contrary, they seem motivated by devotion, respectively, to country and family. Furthermore, if Farinata might indeed be accused of wrongdoing in the part he played in the battle of Montaperti, he shows regret for this: ". . . that noble fatherland to which I was perhaps too harsh" (10.26–27). These words come closer to expressing repentance than those of any other soul in Hell. Moral conscience seems uniquely alive in this soul for whom Virgil, consistently sensitive to righteousness, shows special respect: "And the bold and ready hands of my leader pushed me between the tombs to him, saying: 'Let thy words be fitting' " (10.37–39). At the same time, Cavalcante's lack of concern for himself is equally distinct in the infernal environment. If the proud figure of the one contrasts with the meek and almost pathetic figure of the other, together they generate an atmosphere of noble human sentiments.

What the pilgrim must notice is that neither one seems aware of his own damnation. Farinata's mind is entirely on his city. As for Cavalcante, if he were conscious of Hell, would he not be more concerned about the fate of his son's immortal soul? In fact, although he is still trying to watch over Guido, and is so moving because of this, he is as oblivious to the danger Guido's soul may be in as Farinata is to the emotional scene that interrupts his conversation with the pilgrim. Surely the paternal preoccupation Cavalcante feels beyond the tomb should be primarily for his son's fate beyond the tomb. Would he not want Guido to be spared what he himself is suffering? In different ways these two souls seem to lack awareness of their surroundings and thereby dramatize their intellectual sin of not believing in the world they now belong to. Because they limited their goals to this life by their beliefs, the narrowness of their vision is eternally a part of them, and it is destined to narrow ever more to extinction. As Farinata explains:

> We see, like those with faulty
> vision, things at a distance from us
> . . . ; when they draw near or are
> present our intellect is wholly at
> fault and unless others bring us
> word we know nothing of your human
> state. Thou canst understand,
> therefore, that all our knowledge
> will be dead from the moment the
> door of the future is closed.
> (10.100–108)

Brunetto Latini. Among the violent against nature, the pilgrim meets a revered teacher, Brunetto Latini, in a circle whose vice is probably, although not explicitly, homosexuality. The *Inferno* rarely stresses the sinful actions of the souls who converse at length with the pilgrim, but instead what was hidden in their lives and the disturbing intuitions they awaken in him. It is in this sense that the Brunetto episode is a masterpiece. The pilgrim finds Brunetto, a man of great distinction and intellectual reputation and one for whom he felt personal gratitude and admiration, deep in Hell, naked, scorched, and forced to run continuously to avoid a rain of fire. In order to carry on a conversation, the pilgrim must walk along a wall around the burning sand while Brunetto trots below him. The pilgrim's sense of awkwardness as he tries to assume an attitude of sincere respect toward his teacher whom Hell has stripped of any semblance of dignity, underscores the shock and pain that the encounter causes him. During the conversation Brunetto praises his pupil, expresses confidence in his talents, and prophesies the hardships that political recrimination will bring him, while the pilgrim makes sorrowful protestations of respect and gratitude.

Most moving, but perhaps also most revealing, are the pilgrim's words:

> "Were all my prayers fulfilled" I
> answered him "you had not yet been
> banished from humanity; for in my
> memory is fixed, and now goes to my
> heart, the dear and kind paternal
> image of you when hour by hour in
> the world you taught me how man
> makes himself eternal; and how much
> I am grateful for it my tongue,
> while I live, must needs declare."
> (15.79–87)

The irony here is at first almost incredible: the pilgrim's promise to celebrate his master has resulted in this devastating canto. That he keeps the letter of his promise, to express his own feelings for Brunetto, only adds to the irony. And what of his desire that his teacher had not *yet* been banished from humanity? Does his rather futile wish that Brunetto might be spared Hell for a little longer mask a more heartfelt wish that he himself might be spared the sight of his master's disgrace?

That Brunetto violated something sacred to nature is certain, but it is not clear whether this violation consisted of sexual actions, as most commentaries take for granted, or some more subtle and less physical abuse. Whatever the exact answers, the canto is pervaded by a sense of guilt, irony, and ambiguity, which seem condensed in the pilgrim's haunting words: "hour by hour in the world you taught me how man makes himself eternal" (15.84–85). Is it needlessly cruel for the pilgrim to remind this figure of eternal failure of his earthly lessons on eternity? Perhaps he is speaking more to himself than to Brunetto and, at the same time, he suggests to us that Brunetto's teaching itself may have been how he broke a sacred bond. In the pilgrim's words, *"ad ora ad ora"* ("hour by hour"), we can almost hear the ticking of the clock as Brunetto would often teach how man makes himself eternal, immune from time's passing. Brunetto's ideals, as they are expressed throughout the canto, although intellectually lofty, are ideals of this world: fame, excellence, achievement. But there is no eternity in this world. Did Brunetto somehow teach that there was, that man could rise above his own mortality? Was his teaching a seductive or manipulative lie covered by the dress of the intellectual search for truth and now painfully exposed to the pilgrim in Hell?

Whatever the exact explanation of Brunetto's guilt, this powerful canto's impact depends on our realization that the pilgrim's drama is at its center. Too often we forget that the historical Dante is outside of the poem's action and, in this case, the result can only be that we see his creation as a betrayal of his teacher, missing what it truly represents: his teacher's betrayal of him.

Ulysses. Of all the pockets of Malebolge, the section of Hell containing the sins of fraud, by far the one to which Dante devotes the most space is that of the false counsellors, whose sin is exemplified by two different and major characters. Guido da Montefeltro, the second of the two, tried to obtain salvation through strategy, but found out not only that God demanded good faith, not external gestures, but also that the devils were wise to him as well. A magnificent touch in the episode is to be found in the fact that the only one fooled by Guido's insincere piety was the guileless Saint Francis, who at Guido's death came to take him to Heaven, only to have him snatched away by a devil rightfully claiming his soul. In this limited space it will be necessary, however, to give our more detailed attention to the other false counsellor, regretfully leaving aside Dante's ingenious handling of the subject of human talent corrupted by self-serving ends.

Few figures in the *Divine Comedy* have been so discussed and so admired as Ulysses, the only major character in the *Inferno* who is not from Dante's more or less contemporary world. He is, in fact, not even of the Christian era, but the hero of Homer's Greek epics, known to

Dante only indirectly because, like virtually all of his contemporaries, he did not read Greek. But Ulysses figures prominently in the *Aeneid* as well, not as the hero of the Greek army during the Trojan war, but as the Greek villain who devised the plan that led to the destruction of Troy and the defeat of the Trojan ancestors of the Romans. In both Homer and Virgil, Ulysses is the great strategist of the Trojan war. Whether his role is viewed as good or evil depends on whether it is represented from the Greek or the Trojan point of view. Virgil, whose epic traces the origin of the Romans from the Trojan hero Aeneas, paints a villainous picture of Ulysses. But Virgil also picks up the story of the Trojan war where the *Iliad* leaves off, in a conscious effort to create a Roman epic in the Homeric tradition. Virgil both follows and deviates radically from his model in a relation that is like that of Dante to Virgil himself. Dante's clearest statement of his poem's epic origin comes when he adds his own portrayal of Ulysses to this glorious tradition, by telling a story neither Homer nor Virgil told, the story of how Ulysses died, which was known to no one and, as far as we can tell, was invented by Dante.

Dante's Ulysses did not settle down when, after years of wandering, he finally arrived home to his aged father, his son, and his wife who had waited so loyally and so long for him. The love he had for his family was not strong enough to conquer his passion "to gain experience of the world and of the vices and the worth of men" (26.98–99). Craving further knowledge, he set out with one ship and a few men to explore beyond the Pillars of Hercules, the limit beyond which the gods had forbidden man to travel. His ship took him into the Southern Hemisphere, considered uninhabited in the Middle Ages, where after some time he discovered a mountain higher than any other on earth. But before he was able to land on its shore, a great storm arose and destroyed his ship. He and his men died and he was sent to Hell for the deceitful actions of his life, the best known of which was the invention of the Trojan horse.

Ulysses' story cannot be properly interpreted without consideration of two other stories: that of Aeneas's travels to Italy, and that of Dante's pilgrim's voyage in the *Divine Comedy*. Let us begin with Aeneas. Ulysses could, and probably should, have stayed home with his family after his long travels, but he chose to sail off, relying on his own proverbial craftiness to explore the world beyond the boundaries set by the gods for man's experience. The spirit of Aeneas's travels was the opposite. Aeneas craved a home with his family but, because of the very *pieta*—from the Latin *pietas*, meaning sense of duty in a religious context, the virtue Virgil most frequently associated with Aeneas—that had so little hold on Ulysses (26.94), he endured the hardships of years of travel at the command of the gods. Along the way he lost his wife and his father Anchises and was ordered to leave Dido with whom he had settled down in Carthage. He endured these losses out of obedience to the gods, who had chosen him for the mission of bringing the Trojan seed to Italy and beginning the race destined to found Rome and to rule the world. Aeneas obeyed the gods, sacrificing his personal needs to their providential plan; but Ulysses, relying on his own strength, sought to fulfill his own cravings despite the orders of the gods. The end result was that the one succeeded and founded Rome, while the other failed and went to Hell for his part in the scheme of the Trojan horse, which, ironically, was crucial to the gods' master plan. The founding of Rome, in fact, hinged on the destruction of Troy.

But, if Ulysses' travels contrast with those of Aeneas, so do they, too, with those of Dante's pilgrim. The mountain, in fact, that Ulysses sees is the mountain of Purgatory, to which the pilgrim will arrive after his voyage through Hell, and which he will climb to salvation. Ulysses goes, by a different route and without a guide, to where the pilgrim will be led by a divinely appointed guide. Looking back at the prologue scene when Virgil rescues the pilgrim from the hill, we may remember his words: "Why dost thou not climb the delectable mountain which is the beginning and cause of all happiness?" (1.77–78). Why does Virgil call the hill a mountain? Because, as the pilgrim, on his own strength, sets out to reach the sun at its top, he somehow confuses it with the mountain he will eventually climb, divinely assisted, to his goal. And that mountain is also the very one that Ulysses, following the sun (26:117), discovered and lost simultaneously. The pilgrim cannot yet know this, and neither can the reader, but when he reaches the foot of Purgatory and recognizes Ulysses' mountain, it becomes clear that Ulysses' voyage matches the one the pilgrim might have taken had not Virgil been sent to show him the right way. Aeneas and Dante's pilgrim travel in the footsteps of Providence; Ulysses, on his own strength.

Dante inserts himself into the great classical epic tradition by adding his own to the Greek and Roman stories of Ulysses, the greatest hero common to both Homer and Virgil. He also suggests a unifying principle for the whole tradition, a principle whose logic could be perfected only by his Christian view. The hero of Greece was a destructive villain to the Trojans, but he also forced them to seek a new home in which, as Romans, they were destined by achieve far greater glory. Ulysses is both guilty of and credited with "the ambush of the horse that made the gateway by which the noble seed of the Romans went forth" (26.59–60). This is possible because Providence accomplishes its goals independently of men's intentions, while often using their actions. In Dante's reading, the same Providence that used the Greeks to prepare the road for the Romans used the Romans to prepare the road for Christianity. And so, just as Virgil reworked what Homer had celebrated as the glory of Greece into the hardships endured by Rome's ancestors, so Dante imitates and rewrites Homer's and Virgil's stories as the remote origins of the world in which Christ was to be born.

As Ulysses speaks, Dante joins himself to the Homeric tradition, inviting us to consider the episode not just in relation to the pilgrim, but as involving the *persona* of the poet as well.

> "O brothers," I said "who through a
> hundred thousand perils have reached
> the west, to this so brief vigil of
> the senses that remains to us choose
> not to deny experience, in the sun's
> track, of the unpeopled world. Take
> thought of the seed from which you
> spring. You were not born to live
> as brutes, but to follow virtue and
> knowledge."
>
> (26.112–120)

Ulysses' appeal to his men—an echo of Aeneas's to the Trojans worn-out and discouraged by the hardships and misfortunes of their mission—is an appeal to what Dante once called "the natural thirst" of man, the human desire for knowledge, inseparable from the gift of reason. As Dante wrote this speech he no doubt had in mind his former work, the *Convivio,* whose premise was that man, because he is not an irrational beast, must exert his reason by seeking truth. Although Dante was greatly to qualify this position in the *Purgatorio,* it was held by him for a time as passionately as it is expressed by Ulysses in the famous lines quoted above. It is no wonder that critics have stressed the poet's admiration for Ulysses. He speaks like Dante and as well as Dante. Like Dante, he is endowed with human ideals and with the dangerous gift of eloquence. After his speech his companions, earlier afraid to pass the ominous Pillars of Hercules, were so swayed that he could not have held them back. No matter how idealistic he may have been, he was a danger to himself and to others.

By not recognizing his own limitations, Ulysses used his extraordinary gifts of reasoning and of speech to lead himself and those who followed him toward a goal that they could not accomplish. Dante hopes to avoid this danger by placing his similar gifts under the guidance of the unlimited power that is their source. This is what he means when, at the beginning of the canto, he says:

> I grieved then and grieve now anew
> when I turn my mind to what I saw.
> and more than I am wont I curb my
> powers lest they run where virtue
> does not guide them, so that, if
> favouring star or something better
> have granted me such boon, I may not
> grudge it to myself.
>
> (26.19–24)

Ulysses' journey is not an example of sin—his sin is explicitly stated to be his fraudulent scheming during the Trojan war and does not, in my opinion, include his destructive but sincere swaying of his men—

it is an example of the journey without a guide, avoided by the pilgrim Dante and rejected by the poet Dante.

Ugolino. When the suicide Piero delle Vigne calls himself "just, unjust to myself" (13.72), in some sense he speaks for all of the damned, all of whom acted against their natural inclination toward justice and destroyed their own souls. Because of their humanity, their ruin is personally significant to the pilgrim, who is as they were and could fall as they did. The souls with whom the pilgrim converses at length reveal themselves in such a way as to carry a message and a warning to him. Francesca shows how the imagination can change weakness into self-deceit; Farinata exposes the relative value of virtue without faith; Brunetto's kindness contains disturbing undertones of intellectual seduction; and Ulysses' unguided adventure points to dangers still actual to the poet. These and the other souls in Hell rarely discuss the particular sin that determines their position, nor do they stress publicly known facts about their lives or outwardly visible actions of theirs, but speak rather of things known only to them. They show themselves to the pilgrim, not as they might have been outwardly judged by other men, but as they were inwardly judged by God. And yet, ironically, since they have lost the "good of the intellect," they themselves cannot truly read the intimate message they carry. This message is for the pilgrim who, reflected in them, travels through them into himself, ever more deeply disturbed and awakened within by their dark secrets. No other damned soul has a story more hidden than does Ugolino, whom the pilgrim finds in the deepest part of Hell chewing viciously on the skull of his enemy, Archbishop Ruggieri. At the same time, no soul illustrates better the inability of the damned to read the message revealed by their secrets.

Ugolino, whose crimes were numerous and contemptible, was finally and treacherously put to death for one of which he was probably innocent. He was locked in a tower in Pisa with his four children—in fact, two children and two grandchildren—where he and they were left to starve to death. But, as he himself says, these well-known facts are not his tale, which consists rather in "what thou canst not have learnt" (33.19), that is, what happened inside the prison and inside his soul. Locked in the tower, his paternal instinct to protect and nourish his children was cruelly frustrated during the six days he helplessly watched them starve and then die, one by one. Blinded by hunger, he groped and called for them for two more days and then "fasting had more power than grief" (33.75). Clearly, although not explicitly stated, brutalized by grief and hunger, he ate the flesh of his dead children. The episode is so powerful that we sense no transition between the Hell of Ugolino's last hours on earth and the pain and hatred that he experiences eternally in the deepest and most hidden part of the infernal pit. Literally frozen, he repeats forever the horrible gesture with which his life ended. But the innocent children have disappeared, and the man guilty of their deaths has replaced them as the victim of Ugolino's futile expression of his own brutalization.

This last, and possibly greatest, story of human tragedy in the *Inferno* repeatedly echoes the first, that of Paolo and Francesca, and seems to call the reader to a realization of how deep the pilgrim has traveled. The pilgrim is attracted by the bestial gesture he finds Ugolino engaged in, just as he had been by the light and gentle appearance of the lovers carried together by the wind. He had asked to hear from Francesca her story of love; from Ugolino he asks to hear his story of hatred. Francesca, somewhat insincerely, had claimed that to speak of past happy times would cause her pain; Ugolino warns, most convincingly, that recalling the pain will be almost unbearable for him. Like Francesca, Ugolino agrees to speak, not in the name of love as she had done, but in the hope of causing damage to his enemy. Both are bound eternally to the object of their passion. Finally, the verbal echoes are strong: "There is no greater pain than to recall" (Francesca, 5.121–22); "Thou wilt have me renew desperate grief" (Ugolino, 33.4–5); "I shall tell as one may that weeps in telling" (Francesca, 5.126); "thou shalt see me speak and weep together" (Ugolino, 33.9); "the fair form that was taken from me, and the manner offends me still" (Francesca, 5.101–2); "how cruel was my death, thou shalt hear and shalt know if he has offended me" (Ugolino, 33.20–21). It would seem that the stories are contrasted, the one of love, somehow still with the character, the other of hatred still very much with the sinner. But that is not the effect of Dante's echoes. There is as much love in Ugolino's story of his pain for his children's suffering as there is in Francesca's story of her attraction to Paolo, surely more. And beneath the loving surface of Francesca's story lurks, strikingly like the surface of Ugolino's tale, the unforgiven violence to which it led. Looking back on Francesca from Ugolino, her emotions seem shallow by comparison, perhaps because the pilgrim has reached so much greater depth in his experience.

Although the episode is as strong and direct as anything in Dante's poetry, it causes us to wonder about his intentions. Why at the most corrupt part of Hell do we find the story of innocent victims and of the powerful feelings of a loving father? Why do we find the most basic, natural, and human instincts where we might have expected the greatest perversion? The story of innocent children where we were prepared for corruption? Part of the answer is that corruption is measured by the value of what is corrupted, without which it would have no meaning. The violation by Ugolino's enemies of his humanity as a father and their murder of the guiltless children are profoundly degenerate and dehumanizing actions, whose corruption is dramatized by the bestializing effect it has on Ugolino. But we still wish to make more sense of Ugolino as a character. His guilt is admitted, but not apparent in his last days, in the convincing and selfless father atrociously victimized and abundantly punished for his previous crimes.

To understand better Ugolino's damnation, we must look more closely and pay special attention to the children. Like any soul in the *Inferno*, Ugolino could have been forgiven for his sins by the merciful God who, like the children, was innocent but paid the price of man's sin. Ugolino was certainly not damned for eating his children when, as a human being, to all intents and purposes he was already dead. He was damned for the treacheries of his sinful life before he was locked in the tower. The true point of the unknown story of his last days and hours, a point forever lost to him, is that he failed to turn to Christ, whose signs were everywhere calling to him in the tower. He did not think of Christ when a ray of light made its way into the prison. He did not think of Christ when he looked into the faces of his innocent children and saw his guilty self reflected there. He did not think of Christ when they offered their flesh to him to eat, nor when Christ's dying words echoed so strongly in those of Gaddo: "My father, why dost thou not help me?" (33.69). Dante was counting on his Christian readers to recognize in Ugolino's final act of cannibalism a horrible parody of the Eucharist, held out to Christians each time the Mass is said as a sign of Christ's redeeming sacrifice. Ugolino is in Hell, ultimately like all the other sinners, because he did not accept the mercy Christ offered him.

Satan.

> O Wisdom Supreme, how great is the art
> Thou showest, in Heaven, on earth, and in
> the evil world, and how justly does Thy
> power dispense!
>
> (19.10–12)

God's art in Hell is the art of arranging all that it contains in such a way that its rebellious inhabitants, despite themselves, indirectly point to Him. The concepts of justice and order are very close in Dante's understanding, as are those of sin and disorder. Hell does not correct the sinful as Purgatory does, but it orders them significantly. Their very corruption, through God's art, reveals its true nature as the perversion of what is good. Hell is shaped in nine ever-deeper and ever-decreasing circles leading to the center of the earth. As the pilgrim travels deeper, he witnesses signs of progressive degeneration including always greater distortions of the human form: men turned into trees, heads put on backwards, maimed and swollen bodies and, finally, the "bestial sign" of Ugolino chewing on Ruggieri's head. The pilgrim's sense of pity for what was once human wanes and disappears as he comes upon scenes of ever greater degeneration. But the greatest sign of corruption appears just after Ugolino, in the form of Satan himself, who represents the corruption not just of what was human, but of what was angelic. Satan is monstrously large, dwarfing even the giants the pilgrim mistook earlier for towers; he is covered with hair like an animal; he has bat-like wings whose flapping freezes the bottom of Hell solid with their wind; and possesses three weeping faces smeared with the blood of the three souls he chews and scratches: Brutus, Cassius, and Judas.

Dante's political view, like his moral view, is based on the concept of order, understood as the functioning of each part in accordance with the good of the whole. This order is inevitably conceived as hierarchical, demanding the subjection of the lower to the higher. Within the soul it is manifested by the subjection of the passions to reason, and of the soul to God. Similarly, political order is only fully realized in the form of monarchy, a hierarchy governed by one supreme power at the top, obedient only to God. Where there are many authorities, there are also power struggles and conflicts, the negation of order. The perfect form of government, in Dante's understanding, was a historical reality under the Roman Empire, especially in the age of Augustus. It was not by chance, Dante reasons, that this came about when it did, just before the birth of Christ. Not only was this ideal political state the appropriate place for the birth in time of the eternal God, but its organization, which involved virtually all peoples, facilitated the spreading of the word Christ brought.

Dante attributes the political evils of his day to the absence of an effective monarch to represent God in the secular world, much the same way that the pope represents Him in the Church. The evils that do not come from the absence of an emperor come from the usurping of what should be the emperor's authority by the pope, whose proper domain is the spiritual realm. In an ideal world—and Dante was politically very idealistic—one supreme authority should guide men's lives on earth, the other should guide their souls to Heaven. Augustus, who took the name of Caesar from his adoptive father Julius Caesar, was the first Roman emperor. But Caesar was the general who had brought all of the world under Roman rule and who would have governed it had he not been assassinated by the treacherous Brutus and Cassius. Caesar's relation to the emperor and the empire is in some sense parallel to that of Christ to the pope and the Church. From

Satan's mouths protrude the tormented souls of the betrayers of Caesar and Christ as emblems of treachery against secular and spiritual order and, therefore, against mankind itself. Their intimate relation to Satan is not so much a statement of their own evil as of the sanctity of what they betrayed.

Returning to Satan, who is called "the creature who was once so fair" (34.18), the pilgrim experiences a kind of death as he faces the grotesque figure, or at least a loss of life: "I did not die and I did not remain alive" (34.25). Satan's horrible form marks, in every way, the depth of corruption: "If he was as fair as he is now foul and lifted up his brows against his Maker, well may all sorrow ccome from him" (34.34–36). Situated not only at the bottom of Hell where he rules from below in a parody of the true authority from above, but at the bottom of the universe as well, his massive ugly shape cannot be separated conceptually from the beauty with which he was created, second only to God's. Once the highest angelic spirit, now he is the most material and monstrous of creatures; once the closest to God, now he is the furthest away; originally named after light, now he is the emperor of darkness. Since corruption is as great as what is corrupted, the disgust Satan inspires in the pilgrim comes from the goodness he implies. Like all of Hell, Satan expresses loss, but more so, for his loss is the greatest. And so, in some ironic sense, to look at Satan is to look at the God he once reflected so closely and whom he now parodies with his cross-like shape and his trinitarian heads; it is to see the full force of loss of good, or to look straight at corruption. Virgil has the pilgrim face the horrible spectacle briefly and then guides him on, saying: "we have seen all."

At this point we begin to see that the real universe is like a text of which the pilgrim's path is the reading. Virgil, with the pilgrim hanging onto him, climbs down Satan's body. When he gets to the middle, he turns upside down and begins making his way up the hairy legs and, continuing upward, climbs off the body where, panting, he puts the bewildered pilgrim down. As we find out, the reason for Virgil's reversal of direction is in the place, or more precisely the point, he and the pilgrim have just passed. As a matter of fact, they have not actually reversed their direction as the pilgrim at first thinks: they have merely reversed the position of their bodies, turning upside down in order to continue in the same direction, for the point they have just crossed is the center of gravity.

Although the two travelers will still have to make their way through a kind of tunnel to the surface, they are now already in the Southern Hemisphere, believed by Dante and the Middle Ages to be entirely covered by water. As Dante knew the universe, it was a sphere with the Earth, held together by gravity, at its center. Following Aristotle, he interpreted south as the cosmic upward direction, making the inhabited Northern Hemisphere cosmologically upside down. With these as his principles, he portrays Satan's fall from the heavens as a fall from the uppermost southern part of the universe down as far as descent is possible. Satan was wedged in the center of the world, at the point where any further falling would have been an ascent. Cosmically inverted by the fall, the bottom part of his now massive body protrudes into the Southern Hemisphere, while the top part rules over Hell.

At the time of Satan's fall, the land that had been in the Southern Hemisphere shrank in horror toward the north and was covered over by water, while the land that fled as Satan burrowed his way through the earth rushed up to form the island and the mountain of Purgatory, at the center of the Southern Hemisphere. As Virgil explains to the pilgrim why it was necessary for them to turn upside down in order to continue in the same direction, we, as readers, begin to see that Dante's genius has created a metaphor, the journey of his pilgrim, as broad and as deep as the universe itself. Satan, falling away from God, head first and upside down, fell from the greatest height to the greatest depth and, lodged in the physical center of gravity, formed an inverted spiritual center of gravity, pulling down toward himself all those who, like himself, turned away from God. But, in another larger sense, his position forms the basis of interpretation for the pilgrim's journey, whose downward path it reveals retrospectively to have been upward all along.

When Virgil guided the pilgrim down off the hill leading him by another road, that road seemed to be away from the sun he aspired to, but it is now becoming apparent that it was the true way toward it all along. As John Freccero shows us throughout his works, the journey the pilgrim takes is the concretization of the Augustinian metaphor "descend, so that you may ascend," designed to communicate the Christian message of humility. From our position on Earth, in fact, in Dante's cosmography, if the pilgrim is to take the opposite path from Satan's, he must literally descend in order to ascend. Stated spiritually, this journey is called conversion, from the Latin meaning to reverse positions and, in the middle of Satan's body, Virgil and the pilgrim do exactly this, in order to come out and look up again at the stars.

CHAPTER V

The *Purgatorio*

INTRODUCTION AND PRINCIPLES

The "Allegory of Theologians." The pilgrim leaves the "dead air" of Hell behind and comes out to the sight of the eastern sky brightening just before dawn. The contaminated, enclosed environment of Hell is replaced by the fresh air of the island of Purgatory with the sea gently trembling in the distance. Everything speaks of renewal, of regeneration. Dante announces a poetic resurrection, "here let poetry rise again from the dead" (1.7), in celebration of the pilgrim's passage through death to new life. He has literally left the world of sin behind. He has crossed the center of gravity and turned his body upside down. Virgil has led him up through a downward journey. His voyage, portrayed as unique and spatially defined, is also universal, for it is the spiritual voyage that all Christians take to Christ, through death to new life. The road he lost in the dark wood and failed to find on the hill now stretches before him: "We made our way over the lonely plain, like one who returns to the road he has lost" (1.118–119).

Souls, newcomers like him, arrive carried by a boat from the sea and join him on the beach. They sing of the departure of the Jews from Egypt, in the words of a psalm Dante used elsewhere to explain the principles of allegorical reading of the Bible:

> . . . if we look only at the letter, the meaning given us is the departure of the sons of Israel from Egypt, at the time of Moses; if we

> look at the allegory, the meaning is our redemption brought about
> by Christ; if we look at the moral sense, it is the conversion of the
> soul from the grief and misery of sin to the state of grace; if we look
> at the anagogical sense, it is the departure of the holy soul from the
> bondage of this corruptibility toward eternal glory.
>
> (Letter to Cangrande; my translation)

Dante here illustrates the fourfold method of biblical interpretation
that was typical of the Middle Ages. The four levels—literal or historical, allegorical, moral, and anagogical—are levels or dimensions of
meaning generally applied to the reading of the Old Testament in the
light of the New Testament. Implicit in medieval biblical exegesis is
the assumption that the events of Christ's life are a revelation of eternal truth made temporal and historical. Because Christ is the truth,
He is also the interpretation of all of history and of each man's individual history. His life fulfills and interprets retrospectively the historical facts of the Old Testament and prospectively the life of each man.
As Dante shows in the passage cited earlier, an event in the Old Testament may be read simply as the history of the Jews under God's
protection (literal or historical level), or it may be read as a foreshad-
owing of the revelation of Christ (allegorical level), or it may be read
as a lesson to be used now by any man in his quest for a good life
(moral level). When history, or life, is over, it enters the dimension of
anagogy, from the Greek meaning "the leading up to," that is to say,
it reaches its final result beyond time. In a sense, all of the souls in the
Divine Comedy are their own anagogical interpretations, the final result of their temporal lives.

The history of the chosen people is fulfilled through Christ, whose
death and resurrection, in turn, are reflected in each man's conversion.
In a sense deeply ingrained in the medieval reading of Scripture, each
conversion from sin and each consequent salvation is an Exodus, a
departure of God's people from Egypt. Perhaps nowhere is the insepa-
rability of Dante's allegory from his letter clearer than here on the
regenerative shore of Purgatory, where the pilgrim's and the souls' literal paths meet—the one approaching the realm of grace, the others
eternal glory—as the psalm of the freedom of the Jews from the bondage of Egypt is sung.

Medieval biblical exegesis, studied much more seriously in the last thirty years than before, has been revealed to be radically different from the abstract and arbitrary allegories with which it had been confused. Most frequently, allegory is thought of as a form in which the stated meaning only stands for the real meaning; what is said is not what is meant. Because Dante is clearly concerned with the concept of allegory, his critics have traditionally sought to interpret his poem by the standards of their oversimplified notions. Unfortunate and false platitudes about the *Divine Comedy,* such as Virgil represents human reason or Beatrice represents theology, have been the result of the misunderstanding of Dante's profound relation to medieval biblical exegesis, which he called "the allegory of theologians." While Dante is writing a work of human creation and the "theologians" are interpreting one of divine inspiration, they share the assumption that real events are significant beyond themselves, that levels of meaning are in the nature of reality, not just a device of poets. Ultimately, the fourfold allegories of Scripture were a way of reading history.

For the Middle Ages, the Bible was the historically true and divinely inspired account of events taking place under the protection of Providence. It was given to man so that he could learn of those privileged events and from them of what they point to beyond themselves. The past points to the future, the future interprets the past, and the truth of all events is revealed by Christ, the presence within time of the eternal truth. The most important principle underlying the fourfold method of allegory is, as I have said, that of the revelation of Christ as the means of reading the past and of shaping the present in the light of a teleology beyond time. This principle underlies the nature of Dante's allegory in the *Inferno* and the *Purgatorio* where his fiction is that, like the Bible, the events he tells of really happened and were divinely protected. The relation of his text to Scripture is dramatized with particular emphasis in the scene of the literal meeting of the souls departing from the "Egypt" of this world with the pilgrim departing from the "Egypt" of sin and spiritual death. In a very important sense, the allegory of this literal scene can be defined only as "our redemption brought about by Christ."

By the miraculous parting of the Red Sea the Jews were able to leave the captivity of Egypt but, before they could enter the Promised Land, they had to endure the hardships of crossing the desert. And so the mountain of Purgatory stands like a desert between the pilgrim and the heavenly Jerusalem. Like the souls he meets, he must climb it to strengthen and perfect his commitment and to become truly worthy of the goal at the top.

Cato. Even before the souls arrive, the first sight that occupies the pilgrim's attention is a constellation of four stars:

> I saw four stars never seen before
> but by the first people; the sky
> seemed to rejoice in their flames.
> O widowed region of the north, since
> thou art denied that sight!
> (1.23–27)

The four stars, as Dante makes clear later, are the four cardinal virtues, the virtues that together make up righteousness. Unhappily, the Northern Hemisphere is deprived of this sight, known only to the first people, Adam and Eve. The pilgrim turns around and finds an old man of venerable aspect standing near him, in much the same way as Virgil seemed to appear out of nowhere when the pilgrim turned in fear to run down the hill. The old man's face is lit so brightly by the stars that it is as if the sun itself were shining on him. He is Cato the younger, a Roman traditionally revered for his rigid stoicism and a moral rectitude that finally led him to commit suicide rather than bend to what he perceived as the tyranny of Julius Ceasar.

Cato is the custodian of Purgatory and an immovable reflection of the righteousness symbolized by the four stars that light up the purgatorial sky before dawn. All readers of Dante must wonder why this pagan, suicide, rebel to Caesar is not in Hell. How can he be judged better than the good and gentle Virgil? The reader will no doubt also quickly develop a distaste for him thanks to the high-handed way he treats Virgil and to the lack of emotion he shows for the memory of his wife. Our modern sensibilities are still further offended when we read in our footnotes that among his famous credits was his generosity in first giving his wife to a friend and then, when the friend died, taking her back. But Cato is here because of the virtues traditionally associated with him. He is the perfect Stoic, the man who loves virtue and justice more than he loves his wife, or himself, or life itself. It is Virgil who speaks the words that best interpret Cato in the framework of the *Purgatorio*: "He [the pilgrim] goes seeking liberty, which is so dear, as he [Cato] knows who gives his life for it" (1.71–72). The *Purgatorio* is about freedom; not the freedom of free will, but another freedom that, in his way, Cato embodies and that was lost by Adam and Eve when they lost their home in this right-side-up hemisphere of justice. Free will is the innate freedom to choose good or evil, God or self; but the freedom offered by Purgatory is the moral freedom from the temptation to make irrational choices. The distinction, essential to the doctrine that informs all of the *Purgatorio,* is easier to understand by recalling the example I used to clarify the nature of sin in the *Inferno,* that of the person who breaks his diet out of weakness. While this person makes a free choice in one sense, in another sense he shows himself to be a slave to the irrational desire for the high-calorie food. Cato is Dante's choice of an exemplary figure of self-control; he is the man who would not break his diet.

Despite his moral reputation, Cato is a problematic figure. Even if we can see how his suicide might be interpreted as an act of political martyrdom and how his opposition to Caesar was morally consistent because of the evil he mistakenly saw in him, how do we understand a pagan guarding Purgatory? Ultimately, this is intended to be a mystery, understood only by God. But the fact that Cato is a pagan does have some important thematic relevance to the *Purgatorio.*

Paradoxically, a pagan can in a sense come closer to retrieving what Adam lost than a Christian can, for the highest goal a pagan can strive for is moral. The power to choose right over wrong is innate in all men and fully understood by pagan philosophers who "therefore left ethics to the world" (18.69). Adam did not have to exert self-control because he was created naturally just, with his lower desires spontaneously subjected to his higher ones. When out of pride he sinned, his and all his descendants' desires were disordered, now making it possible for the lower to rule the higher. Indeed, without manly self-control, lower desires constantly pull the soul away from its more rational intentions. But human reason is still relatively intact and it dictates virtue over vice, morally binding man to rational priorities. The pagan's worth or guilt can only be measured in these terms, based on his own strength and commitment to moral good, the highest good achievable by him.

The Christian, however, is not ultimately judged by what he accomplishes, but by what Christ has accomplished for him. All of the souls arriving in Purgatory have made the one all-important choice for Christ, but the weakness and disorder that Adam left mankind as a legacy is still with them. Purgatory does not decide their fate, which has already been decided, but through the discipline of the mountain guarded by Cato, it reorders their desires and restores them to their natural state of justice, making them worthy of the reward they have chosen. No example of a soul saved through Christ could illustrate this intermediary realm's raison d'être as the means of restoring to man the justice that was originally his, symbolized by the light of the four stars that shines so brightly on Cato's Stoic face.

The cardinal virtues and the moral rectitude they stand for are regained through Purgatory, but they are not the way to salvation, as we can see from the numerous examples in the early cantos of the *Purgatorio* of souls who turned to Christ in the last moments of their otherwise sinful lives. "Horrible were my sins" (3.121), says Manfred as he smilingly shows the signs of the disfiguring mortal wounds that brought him to the realization of his need for God's mercy. Jacopo del Cassero did not repent for his "grievous sins" (5.72) until he fell dying and saw his own blood form a pool where he lay. Buonconte da Montefeltro, wounded in the throat, died with the name of Mary in his heart and his arms folded in a cross. None of these souls had even an instant to rectify his life and yet, to the frustration of the devil who came to collect Buonconte, one little tear made the difference between salvation and eternal damnation. It is clear that neither Cato's proverbial virtue nor the justice of the constellation that appears before the sun rises can provide the crucial light of salvation, which is symbolized by the sun. In fact, as we will find out later, the souls in Purgatory must suspend their progress entirely between the setting and the rising of the sun.

Desire. Disordered desire, which "makes the crooked way seem straight" (10.3), is the cause of sin and the mark of fallen nature. It is neither "natural" in the strictest sense nor rational but, because of it, all of Adam's descendants who have chosen Christ must climb the mountain of Purgatory before being united with Him. They must be purged of the sinful inclination that pulls them downward even when their will stretches upward. The mountain will free their natural desire for God from the lesser pull of earthly things, releasing them from a kind of spiritual gravity or heaviness:

> This mountain is such that it is
> always hard at the start below and
> the higher one goes it is less
> toilsome; therefore when it will
> seem to thee so pleasant that going
> up will be as easy for thee as going
> downstream in a boat, then thou
> shalt be at the end of this path;
> there look to rest thy weariness.
> (4.88–95)

The mountain, therefore, expresses the theme of desire or, as it is more often called in the *Purgatorio,* love. The seven terraces between the gates and Eden on the top of the mountain purge the cardinal sins, which are each interpreted as a form of "bad love." Pride, envy, and anger, because they involve the desire for harm to another, express love of something that is not good; sloth expresses insufficient love of what is good; avarice, gluttony, and lust express too much love for something that is good, but that should be loved only proportionately to its limited value. The doctrine of disordered love that Dante presents in the *Purgatorio,* and especially in the middle cantos, is highly influenced by the writings of Saint Augustine. Like Dante, Saint Augustine saw all sin as disordered love. In his preaching, all things are good in principle for, being created by God, they all reflect His glory. However, they should not be loved for themselves, but rather as reflections of their Maker, Who alone is to be loved for Himself. To love anything but God for itself is to turn desire away from its true object, to deviate from good love.

Dante's personal development of Augustine's doctrine includes the pervasive insistence, in a more Thomistic vein, on ordered love as human nature's freedom to be itself. Because of the Fall sin is possible, but it is never natural. The identification by Dante of good love and natural love can be illustrated by one particularly beautiful image, inspired by the sight of the souls purging the prime sin of pride:

> O vainglorious Christians, weary
> wretches who are sick in the mind's
> vision and put your trust in
> backward steps, do you not perceive
> that we are worms born to form the
> angelic butterfly that soars to
> judgement without defence? Why does
> your mind float so high, since you
> are as it were imperfect insects,
> like the worm that is undeveloped?
> (10.121–29)

This magnificent comparison of the soul to the worm that is naturally destined to become a butterfly, turns the traditional dichotomy of the worm and the angel, or the lowliness of human nature and the greatness of the rewards of Heaven, into a natural process. To confess oneself a worm is a traditional manifestation of humility, just as to aspire to a place with the angels is to aspire to the new life after death. Also, to think of salvation can be to marvel, as Augustine did, at God's goodness in transforming our wormlike lowliness into an angelic being. But, with the worlds *"angelica farfalla"* (angelic butterfly), Dante establishes a natural relation between the image of lowliness and that of exaltation. The worm in this image is simply the creature whose potential as a butterfly has not yet been realized. The perversion of sin is not expressed through the image of the worm, whose beautiful flight as a butterfly is the natural development of its humble earthbound motions; rather it is expressed as the unnatural attempt to fly without wings.

Dante's doctrine of love is partly Augustinian, partly Boethian, partly Thomistic, and entirely integrated into his poetic purpose. According to Dante, desire is natural and in man unlimited. Every action is an attempt by the restless soul to possess some good that will satisfy its desire. All motion, all action is love. "Neither Creator nor creature, my son, was ever without love," says Virgil (17.91–92). Natural love, which is the compulsion of all things to act according to their natures, is always good. Different from lower creatures, man also has "chosen love" (*amor d'animo*), which never errs as long as it focuses on the prime good (God), desiring all other things only according to their value. The soul strays when it gives too much value to secondary goods, or too little to the primary one, or otherwise distorts the value of the object desired. Again, we can use one of Dante's images to clarify the essence of his doctrine:

> From His hand who regards it fondly
> before it is, comes forth, like a
> child that sports, tearful and
> smiling, the little simple soul that
> knows nothing, but, moved by a
> joyful Maker, turns eagerly to what
> delights it.
>
> (16.85–90)

This stunning image of the newly created soul as an infant with no intellectual content save the desirability of good and no form of expression except joy at pleasure and unhappiness at pain, clearly reflects Dante's position that, although corruptible, human nature is not corrupt. The natural desire that propels it is ultimately for God's goodness. But the goodness inherent in all created things and their relative desirability can cause the soul to stray, to deviate from greater good toward lesser good. Hence the need for discretion and self-discipline in the individual, and good government in society. Some natural desires must be controlled in the light of higher and ultimately more natural desires: "To a greater power and to a better nature you, free, are subject," says Marco Lombardo (16.79–80). True submission is true freedom and this "free submission" is the goal of Purgatory.

Very close to Boethius, Dante describes an insatiable desire created in the human soul that, he will tell us in the *Paradiso,* is not destined to frustration. But neither can it be satisfied by any good short of the Absolute. All too often man's earthly existence is a continuous quest for what, even when possessed, can only leave him still searching. False goals, objects he selects to make him happy, to fulfill him, include not only material goods, but other desirables as well, such as fame, honor, or even knowledge. These objects of desire are deceptive in that they are not the prime good and therefore cannot satisfy man's unlimited craving. Possession of them, in fact, does not bring happiness but only the desire for more. In other words, human desire is often simply the expectation of happiness from an object that cannot fulfill that expectation.

Imagination. A central theme of the *Purgatorio* is that, although we have the rational power of discrimination ("*virtù che consiglia*" [18.62]) to help us follow our natural desires in due measure, our imagination drives us to love in undue measure.

> Your perception takes from outward
> reality an impression and unfolds it
> within you, so that it makes the
> mind turn to it; and if the mind, so
> turned, inclines to it, that
> inclination is love, that is nature,
> which by pleasure is bound on you
> afresh. Then, as fire moves upward
> by its form, being born to mount
> where it most abides in its matter,

> so the mind thus seized enters into
> desire, which is a spiritual
> movement, and never rests till the
> thing loved makes it rejoice. Now
> may be plain to thee how hidden is
> the truth for those who maintain
> that every love is in itself
> praiseworthy . . .
>
> (18.22–35)

Just as fire moves upward, so the soul bends toward what it appre-
hends with pleasure, acting out its primary instinct of love. But the
soul does not turn directly to the "outward reality," the object in itself;
instead it turns to the presentation of reality it receives, to the way the
imagination introduces or "unfolds" it. The dominant role of the
imagination in desire becomes most apparent in the symbolic dream
immediately following the cantos dedicated to the exposition of the
doctrine of love (cantos 15–18).

In his dream the pilgrim sees a stammering, ugly, deformed, and
mutilated woman turn into a beautiful siren singing an irresistible
song of love. Then a holy lady appears, rebukes Virgil for his lack of
vigilance and, inspired by her, Virgil rips the clothes off the siren, exposing at once her belly and such a powerful stench that the pilgrim
is awakened by it. Although there are many hypotheses about the
identity of the "holy lady" (Lady Philosophy, Beatrice, Saint Lucy), the
message is perfectly clear. The siren is a seductive illusion from which
the combination of the lady and Virgil are able to defend the pilgrim's
soul.

With this dream, Dante gives us an unusual version of the com-
monplace way of representing the joys of this world as a seductive
woman. Usually the siren is presented as dangerous but beautiful or,
more precisely, dangerous because of her beauty. However, this siren
has no beauty; indeed, she is a pathetic collection of imperfections:
stammering tongue, crooked eyes and legs, lost hands, and unhealthy
color. She does not have the means or even the desire to seduce the
pilgrim. Instead, his own imagination supplies the means of seduction:

> I gazed at her, and as the sun
> revives cold limbs benumbed by the
> night, so my look gave her a ready
> tongue and then in a little time
> made her quite erect and coloured
> her wan features as love desires.
> When she had her speech thus set
> free she began to sing so that it
> would have been hard for me to turn
> my mind from her.
>
> (19.10–19)

"As love desires." The siren is not dangerous until the pilgrim sees in her what he wants to see, what his imagination gives her. Then she sings her lying song:

> "I am," she sang, "I am the sweet
> siren who beguiles the sailors in
> mid-sea, so great delight it is to
> hear me. I turned Ulysses, eager on
> his way, to my song, and he who
> dwells with me rarely departs, so
> wholly I content him."
>
> (19.19–24)

According to medieval doctrines of love, it is because the imagination feeds passion that the way to resist unhealthy desire is to refrain from dwelling on the object of pleasure. For, as Dante shows with his dream, the passage from pleasure, or even mild interest, to obsession is through the imagination. The final phase of the dream is perhaps the most intriguing part. The unclothing of the siren surely represents much more than the exposing of her objective value. We do not have a return to the unfortunate figure who appeared originally in the dream and was the "outward reality," but a new and much more horrible creature lurking behind the lies with which the imagination has covered her. This creature is corruption disguised as fulfillment. As Virgil exposes the lower part of the so-desired female body, the smell, perhaps of rotting flesh or death, awakens the pilgrim at once from his passion and his dream. In this remarkable passage, Dante is not preaching against the flesh; rather, he is representing the power of the imagination to endow its object of desire with false promises of fulfillment. Without these lies, physical beauty is helpless to seduce man away from the true source of fulfillment that it reflects.

In this same canto the pilgrim meets a figure who further clarifies the message developed over the middle cantos. This is Adrian V, whose life has extraordinary value as a paradigm. Adrian's craving for riches and power was virtually insatiable and so, never satisfied by what he gained, he strove to obtain ever more, and finally rose to the papacy and the possesion of as much power and wealth as is available on earth. When he came to possess everything, the lie of all earthly things finally hit him. His heart was still not at rest, and his conversion coincided with the rational discovery that happiness is not of this world. Adrian's craving was that natural love that is given us as our prime instinct, but he was corrupt as long as he saw its fulfillment in the things of this world. He was blessed with the direct experience of the powerlessness of limited objects to satisfy unlimited longing.

Passion is an obsession manipulated by the imagination. The purpose of the mountain is to train the desire to obsession with its proper object. God is already chosen and desired by the souls in Purgatory, but the mountain will only release them when that desire becomes their exclusive passion. In the *Purgatorio* the role of the imagination is central. Dreams, visions, images, disembodied voices, paradoxical experiences of the senses and an existence dedicated to desire, make up the experience of the souls and of the pilgrim. If, in the *Inferno*, God's art is expressed through real lives that, despite their intentions, carry a saving message of justice, His art in Purgatory is, like human art, through the appeal to the imagination. The souls themselves are presented as a mysterious form of illusion. They have the appearance of bodies, they even experience sensations such as pain and hunger. However, the pilgrim is soon made aware of their lack of concreteness when he attempts in vain to embrace Casella on the shore of Purgatory. It should be remembered that the souls in Hell do not have bodies either and will not have them until the Day of Judgment but, poetically, they are treated exactly as if they did, for Dante wants us to imagine the weight, the corporality, and the real and eternal presence of the infernal souls. The point of narrative fact that the souls have no bodies becomes a poetic theme only in the *Purgatorio,* the *cantica* of desire and imagination.

PURGATORY'S POETS

Sordello. Were there no other reason to view Purgatory as the realm of the imagination (and there are many besides the ones already discussed), we might be led to such a view just by the preponderance of souls of artists and poets found on the mountain: Casella, Oderisi, Sordello, Statius, Forese, Bonaggiunta, Guinicelli, Arnaut to name only the principal ones and not to mention others like Cimabue, Giotto, and Cavalcanti whose works are discussed. Of the pilgrim's many encounters with artists, two stand out: those of Sordello and Statius. Both extend over several cantos, both include essential digressions and, above all, both derive their power and their significance from the presence in them of the figure of Virgil.

Just before Virgil's and the pilgrim's meeting with Sordello a curious, and I think momentous, exchange occurs between the two:

> I began: "It seems to me, O my
> light, that thou deniest expressly
> in one passage that prayer bends the
> decree of heaven, and for this alone
> these people pray. Will their hope,
> then, be vain, or are thy words not
> rightly clear to me?"
>   And he said to me: "My writing
> is plain and the hope of these souls
> is not mistaken, if thou consider
> well with sound judgement; for the
> height of justice is not lowered
> because the fire of love fulfils in
> a moment the satisfaction due from
> each who sojourns here, and in the
> place where I set down that point

defect was not made good by prayer
because the prayer had no access to
God.

(6.28–42)

The pilgrim's problem is brought about by the assault on him of souls requesting him to shorten their sentence in Purgatory by seeking prayers for them on earth. But he remembers a line of the *Aeneid* that states that prayers cannot bend the will of the gods. It is hard to see where the problem is. Souls in Purgatory, in accordance with Church teaching, clearly believe that prayer has the power to obtain additional mercy for them and a pagan text denies such flexibility in pagan gods. If the *Aeneid* were an authoritative religious text, then the problem would be clear; but it is a pagan poem. Why does the pilgrim not simply dismiss Virgil's line as false? Why does he need to understand how it is not contradicted by Christian truth? Virgil answers, not as we should expect, that his text is false or even that the pagan gods of whom he was speaking were false, but rather that the characters in it, being pagan, were at fault.

From this passage we can only conclude that the *Aeneid* is in some way an infallible text whose authority is comparable to that of the Bible. It has, in fact, been called Dante's "Bible of the Empire," largely because of the authority he attributes to it as the account of the beginnings of the Roman Empire, which in turn he understands as a privileged history guarded by Providence. Virgil's role as poet of the Roman Empire gives him the status of a secular prophet. This is surely true, but not an exhaustive explanation of the unique value that Dante gives Virgil in the *Divine Comedy*. Virgil, "the gentle sage, who knew all" (*Inferno* 7.3), seems to dramatize a virtually perfect vision of the world without the revelation brought by Christ just nineteen years too late for him. Just as the Roman Empire prepared the perfect secular setting for God's great act of mercy, so Virgil seems to comprise whatever is humanly possible before or without the state of grace. He is both wise and fallible, both innocent and unredeemed. Any formula can only limit the richness of this character, created by Dante from his cherished reading of the greatest poem known to him.

When the two travelers first see Sordello, a thirteenth-century Christian poet and patriot, he is isolated and appears almost antisocial. When asked for directions, instead of complying, he questions them on where they are from. But, as Virgil begins to identify himself and his homeland, he gets no further than the name of his city, Mantua, before Sordello leaps up to embrace him because he, too, is from Mantua. At this point Dante interrupts the action to exclaim at length on the sad state of Italy, torn apart at every level by conflict among its citizens. Dante's lengthy and rightly famous invective continues for the rest of the canto, while the brotherly embrace of the poet compatriots is almost suspended and momentarily frozen into an emblem of the harmony between citizens so essential to society and so betrayed by the guilty citizens and leaders of Dante's Italy. When the action picks up again, Virgil identifies himself and again Sordello embraces him, this time not as a brother, but humbly around the knees, "where the inferior does."

> "O glory of the Latins," he said
> "through whom our tongue showed
> forth its power, O eternal honour of
> the place from which I come, what
> deserving or what grace shows thee
> to me?"
>
> (7.16–19)

The theme of nationalism has not only not been abandoned, it has been deepened, for belonging to the same land implies more than a geographical or political sharing: it implies a cultural and linguistic bond, a common heritage. As Sordello, moved and reverent, kneels before Virgil, Dante's poem itself seems to pause for a moment of homage and tribute to a poet whose human effort has left behind an unequaled treasure for the generations that followed him. We are reminded of the pilgrim's awed and humble response when he first met Virgil and it is clear that, as Statius will do later, Sordello here speaks not just for himself, but for Dante as well. Furthermore, the devout wording of Sordello's homage, "*gloria*" (glory), "*pregio etterno*" (eternal praise), *"grazia"* (grace), suggests a sacred object of praise. Still, we would miss the point if we failed to appreciate that this moment of unqualified homage is sandwiched between explicit references to Virgil's exclusion from salvation because of the chronological contingency of his death occurring before the birth of Christ, "the Sun above for which thou longest and which was known by me too late" (7.26–27).

Night falls and Sordello explains that, once the sun has set on Purgatory, no forward progress is possible until it rises again the following morning. The symbolism is, of course, clear: without the light of Christ all of man's efforts are hopeless. Where does that leave the "glory of the Latins"? The poignancy of Virgil's figure in the poem is never greater than when he anxiously asks for further explanation of what, for everyone else involved, is simply an easily acceptable rule. If someone wanted to move upward on the mountain, asks Virgil, what would happen? Would he be stopped by some outside power or would his own forces abandon him? Sordello simply draws a line on the ground and tells Virgil that, once the sun has set, he could not so much as step over the line. The reason is nothing else but the darkness itself, the absence of the light. In effect, what Virgil asks is what would happen if someone tried, and the answer is, mysteriously, that he could not try. Virgil backs off, resigned but still wondering. This powerful scene prepares the way for the beautiful sight that will soon appear in the darkened sky and draw the pilgrim's hungry eyes to itself: the constellation of the theological virtues, brightly shining where that of the cardinal virtues had been in the morning. Without faith, hope, and charity, Virgil, the epitome of human worth, cannot cross a line drawn on the ground. But the point of Dante's message is the other side of the coin, the regenerative light of the constellation that restores the great worth that Adam lost for all men.

Statius.

> Men yonder still speak my name,
> which is Statius; and I sang of

Thebes and then of great Achilles,
but fell by the way with the second
burden. The sparks that kindled the
fire in me were from the divine
flame from which more than a
thousand have been lit—I mean the
Aeneid, which was in poetry my
mother and my nurse; without it I
had not weighed a drachm, and to
have lived yonder when Virgil lived
I would have consented to a sun more
than I was due before coming forth
from banishment.

(21.91–102)

The souls in Purgatory crave their freedom from the mountain
and this craving increases until it is so pure that the "religion of the
mountain" no longer holds them, for their desire is now in total accord
with their will. Statius, the soul speaking above, has just been released
and yet, paradoxically, he expresses the willingness to trade his freedom, or at least to delay it, for something else: to have known Virgil,
the man without whose poetry his could not have been, on Earth. His
statement is not only paradoxical; if taken literally, it is perverse, for
to "have lived yonder when Virgil did" would have meant to have been
excluded from Heaven altogether, as Virgil himself was. Indeed, Statius's chronology is as fortunate as Virgil's is unfortunate, for just as
Virgil died a few years before the birth of Christ, so Statius was born
only a few years after Christ's death, a fact that Dante exploits by
inventing a chronologically possible conversion for him.

The encounter between Virgil and Statius is, in fact, paradoxical
throughout. Statius honors Virgil not only as the source of his poetry,
but also as the one who saved him from vice and, finally, as the reason
he became a Christian:

Thou didst like him that goes by
night and carries the light behind
him and does not help himself but

makes wise those that follow,. . .
Through thee I was poet, through
thee Christian.

(22.67–69, 73)

Statius seems to have derived everything from Virgil and, considering
the debt he owes, his extravagant reverence does not seem out of
place, especially since, as a reflection of Virgil, Statius is pale indeed.
We need only consider that, by his own admission, the reason his poetry nowhere expresses his Christian faith is because, living in an age
when Christians were persecuted, he was afraid to be a public believer.
Perhaps this is the most significant paradox of all. Virgil showed others the way to Christ without knowing Him, while Statius knew Christ
but intentionally suppressed His message. Virgil stands in darkness
showing the light, while Statius stands in the light and shows only the
darkness of paganism.

Although some readers and critics are so astounded by the seeming unfairness of Virgil's position in eternity compared to that of Statius that they can perceive only irony in this great encounter, I think
we must search further for Dante's intention. First and foremost, how
could he more strongly dramatize the crucial nature of what took
place in the few years between Virgil's death and Statius's birth than
by the salvation of a figure as limited as Statius as a result of Christ's
atoning death and the exclusion of one as great as Virgil without it?
Virgil is somehow a way to measure human worth. None is better,
none is wiser, and no poetic text is more revealing. But human worth
is not enough.

One aspect of the reverence shown to Virgil by the pilgrim, by
Sordello, and by Statius, is their dependence. Their work is somehow
sired by his; without him they could not have been; he is their source,
their origin, the way they explain their activity in the art that "most
honors and most endures." Virgil represents the fullness of humanity
ready for redemption but standing just short of it. He is the blooming
of the pagan world that will die at the birth of the Christian one and
the personal father of the human art practiced by Dante, Sordello, and
Statius. Or perhaps we might better say he is the mother ("my mother

74

and my nurse"), for he offers the ground in which the seed is about to be sown. As Statius explains:

> Already [so short after Virgil's
> death] the world was everywhere big
> with the true faith, sown by the
> messengers of the eternal kingdom,
> and thy words I have just spoken
> were so in accord with the new
> preachers that I formed the habit of
> visiting them.
>
> (22.76–81)

Virgil reflects that world just before the seed was planted. The humanity to which Christ brought life is somehow embodied in the expressive richness of Dante's portrayal of Virgil. It is as if Dante were saying man cannot understand himself without this "divine flame," but he cannot be fulfilled without Christ. Virgil is powerless to fill the gap between his death and the birth of Statius. He cannot cross the line drawn by Sordello on the ground for, ultimately, without Christ, human potential is sterile. The extraordinary combination of fertility and sterility in Virgil makes of him a figure that rivals the great heroes of pathos in Virgil's own poem.

Statius's Conversion. Dante, Sordello, and Statius are bonded to Virgil by their reading of the *Aeneid,* by the nourishment Virgil's poetry gives them. The homage to Virgil is finally a reading of his poem and the Statius episode is primarily about the nature of that reading, perhaps of any reading. During the course of their conversation, Statius alludes to two places in Virgil's poetry particularly significant for his conversion. The first of these led to his moral conversion. Although he is now in the terrace of avarice, his sin on earth was not avarice but its opposite: prodigality or wastefulness of riches. In the Aristotelian ethical tradition, Dante views virtue as right measure and vice as excess. To one virtue correspond two opposite vices. Just as, for example, the opposite of courage is both foolhardiness and cowardice, prodigality and avarice are both opposite to generosity. Statius explains to Virgil that because he did not realize that too much spending was a vice of the same nature as hoarding, he might very well have died morally corrupt, had Virgil's words not brought him to the realization of the wrongness of excessive spending. What stands out in this passage is that the Italian rendering of the Virgilian lines appears to be a mistranslation. The Italian means: "Why, oh rightmeasured desire for gold, do you not control the appetite of mortals?" But the Latin means: "To what extremes, oh cursed hunger for gold, do you not drive the appetite of mortals?" The Italian rendering is, grammatically, a possible understanding of the Latin, but, given the context in the *Aeneid,* certainly a wrong one.

This passage has been a problem to Dante critics, some of whom conclude that Dante misunderstood the line, while others try to reread the Italian so that it fits the Latin, somehow to justify the mistranslation as a kind of extension of the meaning of the Latin. But, the fact is that the line, if read correctly, could not have the message that was so vital for Statius. In fact, while Statius was aware that avarice was a vice, he had not realized that an excess of generosity could also be a vice. The Virgilian lines express outrage at the betrayal of a friend for money and in no way suggest the principle of virtue as the right measure between opposite excesses. It seems that only through a misreading of the line itself, understanding the word *"coqis"* to mean "control" rather than "drive" and the word *"sacra"* to mean "sacred" or "venerable" rather than "fearsome," could Statius be enlightened about the moral danger in which he was living. If this is so, then either Dante misread the line or Statius did; that is, either our poet made a mistake or he intentionally represented Statius as making one. Most Dante critics have learned to turn to error on the part of this poet as a last resort. Surely here, where we are dealing with a text so intimately known by Dante, this principle should be invoked. If so, then Statius learned a crucial lesson by misreading a line in Virgil.

Perhaps Dante's intention is to stress the line's importance not so much in its original context as in the context of Statius's reading. When Statius read that line he understood and changed the direction of his life. Perhaps in order to make his point about the nature of the literary message, Dante chooses to exemplify it with what is, in the ordinary sense, a misreading. This way we cannot mistake finding a message in a text for understanding its words. Statius's moral conversion ("and I repented of that as of my other sins" [22.44–45]) upon reading, correctly or incorrectly, a line of poetry reminds us of Francesca's fall:

> Many times that reading drew our
> eyes together and changed the colour
> in our faces, but one point alone it
> was that mastered us; when we read
> that the longed-for smile was kissed
> by so great a lover, he who never
> shall be parted from me, all
> trembling, kissed my mouth. A
> Galeotto [pander] was the book and he that
> wrote it; that day we read in it no
> farther.
>
> (*Inferno* 5.130–38)

Despite Francesca's blaming of the author, he could not possibly have intended this particular effect for the celebrated passage in which, as a matter of fact, it is Guinevere who kisses Lancelot not, as Francesca would have it, the other way around. While Francesca surrenders to passion and Statius turns away from vice, in both cases a line of poetry, removed from its literary context, comes to play a crucial role in their lives.

The great precedent for Dante's representation of so dramatic a role played by a sudden encounter between a reading and an experience is one of the most famous scenes in Western literature, the conversion of Saint Augustine:

> I seized it [the book] and in silence I read the first passage on which my eyes fell: *Not in revelling and drunkenness. Not in lust and wantonness. Not in quarrels and rivalries. Rather, arm yourself with the Lord Jesus Christ; spend no more thought on nature and nature's appetites.* I had no wish to read more and no need to do

so. For in an instant, as I came to the end of the sentence, it was as
though the light of confidence flooded into my heart and all the
darkness of doubt was dispelled.[3]

Statius's misreading of the lines in Virgil is an exaggerated version
of the concept of the reader's receptiveness as an inescapable aspect of
the text, a concept also very relevant to Dante's Christian reading of
the *Aeneid*. We are told too often of the distorted readings the Middle
Ages gave to the pagan classics that, we are informed, only regained
their autonomy with the Renaissance. But Christian readings of pagan
texts should not always, and certainly not in the case of Dante, be
dismissed as gratuitous twistings of meaning. As Dante would see it,
a reader in possession of the light of Christ's word would use that truth
to contribute to his understanding of any other and necessarily lesser
truth. The light it sheds on his reading increases his understanding; it
does not cloud it. This is a principle most of us apply to our reading
of the *Divine Comedy* itself, recognizing the value of Dante's vision
within its spiritual and ideological context and, at the same time, seeking out its relevance to our ideologies and beliefs as well as to our
doubts.

Virgil's Pagan Vision. Most often cited as an example of the medieval approach to interpretation of the classics is the Christian reading of Virgil's *Fourth Eclogue*. The *Fourth Eclogue* announces the
birth of a baby who will bring back the Golden Age to Earth. Justice
and innocence will return and human guilt will disappear. While Virgil
was merely celebrating the birth of a friend's son with a piece of
Golden Age poetry, according to many moderns, the common medieval reading of this eclogue was as a prophecy of the coming of Christ.
The Golden Age is a common theme of ancient poetry based on a myth
of cosmic cycles whereby the world begins harmonious, innocent, and
pure but progressively degenerates toward chaos only to be born again
in a new Golden Age. The Golden Age is the cyclic rebirth of the world
in pristine order. Exactly what Virgil is doing in the *Fourth Eclogue* is
not clear, but he seems to be celebrating the birth of a child, hyper-
bolically announcing it as a cosmic event. Why the Middle Ages might

see this as a prophecy of the birth of the Baby Savior is clear. But that it was, in fact, widely taken in the Middle Ages to be a prophecy is a greatly exaggerated statement. Medieval students of Virgil often associated the poem with the birth of Jesus, but they rarely believed it was written as a prophecy of it.

In the case of Statius, it was in fact the *Fourth Eclogue* that led him to become a Christian, but not by its revealing Christ to him. Statius so admired Virgil that, when he realized that the preaching of the Christians resembled some of Virgil's words, he took interest in them, went to hear them, and learned from them of Christ. By the quality of his humanity and poetry Virgil led Statius to the truth that he himself could not see. Statius owes his conversion and his salvation to Virgil's words, but those words mediate conversion and salvation, they do not provide them. Statius must know of Christianity in order to see it in the Virgilian lines. Similarly, a Christian cannot read the lines without seeing Christian truth reflected in them. Dante's reading of all of Virgil is based on this assumption. Virgil sang of the world as it became ready for Christ, without knowing that Christ would come. But his Christian reader can see, in that world of promise and despair, readiness for what was about to happen.

In regard to the Roman Empire, it is clear how Dante reads the *Aeneid.* Virgil celebrates a privileged moment in history under the Emperor Augustus, and he celebrates it as the culmination of a plan ordained by the father of the gods, Jupiter, to bring about a great age of peace, prosperity, and Roman government in all the world. This was Jupiter's unchangeable design as far back as the Trojan war, when he chose to bring the Trojan stock, in the person of Aeneas, to Italy to mix its blood with that of the Latins and begin what was to be the Roman race. In all of this, Dante takes the *Aeneid* as authority. However, as I have said before, the divine plan to which Virgil testifies extends beyond what he could have known, because the glory of the Roman Empire is only a preparation for the coming of Christ.

The *Aeneid* is an epic, but it is also a powerful combination of celebration and despair. Alongside the triumph of Rome, over and over we witness the poet's bitterness at the senseless tragedy of young men and young women suffering and dying as the victims of small mistakes and capricious destiny. Perhaps the most famous and surely the most significant example of Virgil's attitude toward such human loss is the brief episode of Marcellus in book 6. Aeneas visits the underworld where he is able to speak with Anchises and, by gaining understanding of the importance of his own role as father of the Roman race, somehow to mature beyond dependence on his father. In order to give firm direction to his son and to reassure him of the purposefulness of his hardships and suffering, Anchises shows him the unborn souls of the great Roman heroes and tells him of the future glories of his race. This episode furnishes Virgil with the opportunity for his strongest exaltation of the Rome of his time and of the events that led up to it. But, at the very end of the survey of the great Romans and the greatness of Rome, Aeneas notices "a young man beautifully formed and tall in shining armor." Reluctantly and weeping, Anchises tells him that this is the young Marcellus who will be the greatest of the Romans but who, because of his premature death, will be tragically robbed of the opportunity to realize his unequalled potential.

> Fate will give earth only a glimpse of him,
> Not let the boy live on. Lords of the sky,
> You thought the majesty of Rome too great
> If it had kept these gifts . . .
> . . . .
> Child of our mourning, if only in some way
> You could break through your bitter fate. For you
> Will be Marcellus. Let me scatter lilies,
> All I can hold, and scarlet flowers as well,
> To heap these for my grandson's shade at least,
> Frail gifts and rituals of no avail.[4]

In Virgil's text, Marcellus stands as a symbol of the individual suffering and loss that cannot be repaid even by the triumphs and glory of Rome. As Virgil celebrates Rome and many of the Stoic ideals of his day, he never forgets, or allows his reader to forget, that he has found no answer to the human suffering that he repeatedly represents as the death of the very young and their loss to the mature. Individual nobility, beauty, and virtue do not seem to sway the merciless gods against whom the poet raises his voice in bitterness and hopelessness.

Dante, who certainly took the *Aeneid* as a sincere celebration of the greatness of Rome, was also sensitive to the bitterness that is so much a part of it. But this too, in his mind, reflected the age in which Virgil lived. In fact, Christ had not yet brought to earth the answer to Virgil's tormented questions. Stoicism promised only cosmic providence and accepted individual sacrifice as inevitable, but Christianity offered salvation to each man and promised justice to each life, not in this world but in the next. In Dante's reading, the despair of Virgil's poetry signifies humanity's need for the good news that was to come, as does his eternal position in Limbo, and his replacement by Beatrice.

THE TOP OF PURGATORY

The Arrival of Beatrice. The romantic reader expecting the pilgrim's reunion with his lover to be a triumph of human love and desire over time and death will be disappointed by Beatrice's arrival. But an admirer of Dante's medieval poetry can never cease to marvel at the dimensions of significance that accompany the long-awaited moment. Beatrice's arrival is preceded by a procession composed of characters symbolizing the books of Scripture, with the Old Testament in front of the New Testament and with a cart, symbolizing the Church, dividing them. The cart is drawn by a griffin, the legendary animal half lion and half eagle, standing for Christ and accompanied by seven nymphs representing the cardinal and theological virtues. The procession's symbolism is obvious, but the modern reader might well miss its meaning. Scripture, for the Middle Ages, is the divinely guided account of all of history, from the Creation at the beginning of time to the end of time and Judgment Day. What passes before the pilgrim is therefore all of history, or time itself. This procession of history stops as the cart drawn by the griffin arrives in front of him and all of the members of the procession ahead of the triumphal cart—that is, those symbolizing the books of the Old Testament—turn around and face the central part. The centrality of Christ in history is dramatized by this turning toward Him of what went before and of what was to follow and still is to follow Him. As part of the pilgrim's experience, this representation of all history is presented personally to him, suggesting, among other things, the Christian analogy between the coming of Christ for all men and His coming in the life of each man. But the relationship between universal history and the pilgrim's personal history or experience takes a dramatic turn with what follows. The whole procession looks toward the cart, in expectation of some final event that can incontrovertibly be identified as the second coming of Christ at Judgment Day. Angels announce what seems to be the arrival of Christ with the words: "*Benedictus qui venis*" (30.19). But, on the background of a dawnlike sky awaiting the sun, amidst showers of flowers and light, and songs of triumph, what emerges from the cart is not Christ but Beatrice, and she arrives not to embrace her lover but to judge him.

At this point, a digression on the relation of Beatrice to Christ is necessary. As far back as the *Vita Nuova* Dante applied theological and Christological imagery to Beatrice. In the *Vita Nuova* the number nine, consistently connected to Beatrice's appearances, reflects her miraculous nature. Dante explains that the multiplication of three by itself represents the Trinity acting on its own power, without the mediation of nature. A mircle is, in fact, a supernatural event above the laws of nature, a direct intervention of the divinity into the world. When Dante calls Beatrice a miracle, he is referring to the miraculous effect she has on his life, analogous to that of Christ on universal history. Through Beatrice's association with the number nine, her name ("the one who makes blessed"), through the importance of her greeting, whose etymological connection to salvation is stressed, and through many other details of the *Vita Nuova,* Dante represents Beatrice as the saving grace in his life, sent by God as Christ was, and returned to God through her death, as Christ was. And now, as Christ will, she comes back to the pilgrim's life for the second and final time, bringing salvation and judgment.

Before passing on to Beatrice's judgment of the pilgrim at this final stage of his dramatized personal history, let us look at something else that coincides with this remarkable moment. As the procession stands poised in expectation of Beatrice's arrival, a hundred angels, "messengers of eternal life" (30.18), cry out:

> "*Benedictus qui venis,*"
> and, scattering flowers upward and around
> "*Manibus, oh, date lilia plenis.*"
> (30.19–22)

"*Manibus date lilia plenis*" ("scatter lilies, all you can hold"), is the only direct untranslated quotation from Virgil in the *Divine Comedy.* As we have seen, it refers to the "ritual of no avail" that the disconsolate Anchises invoked for the young Marcellus. The inclusion of Virgil's text at this point could hardly be more significant. Messengers of eternal life celebrate what seems to be the arrival of Christ with the words the pagan poet used to express, admist the triumph of Rome, the tragedy of human life. Virgil's "ritual of no avail" has become the announcement of "eternal life," or the resolution of his tragic vision. But this is not all. The arrival of Beatrice, announced as if it were the coming of Christ, coincides not only with the disappearance of Virgil as a character from the poem, but also with the pilgrim's consequent almost Virgilian sense of abandonment and loss, so much like that of Aeneas at Anchises' death.

As Beatrice appears, with her face still hidden by a veil, the pilgrim recognizes her presence by the overpowering response he has to it, never provoked in him by anything except her. Her familiar powerful effect, which he has not felt for so long, fills him with fear. As he turns to Virgil for comfort, the poet turns to Virgil's poetry, where Dido apprehensively expresses the feelings Aeneas has awakened in her, feelings she has not experienced since the death of her husband:

> I shall say it: since that time
> Sychaeus, my poor husband, met his fate,
> And blood my brother shed stained our hearth gods,
> This man alone has wrought upon me so
> And moved my soul to yield. *I recognize*
> *The signs of the old flame,* of old desire.
> (*Aeneid* 4.20–23; my italics)

Dante's pilgrim unequivocally recalls Virgil's heroine:

> And my spirit, which now so long had
> not been overcome with awe,
> trembling in her presence, without
> having more knowledge by the eyes,
> through hidden virtue that came from
> her, *felt old love's great power.*
> As soon as the lofty virtue smote on
> my sight which already had pierced
> me before I was out of my boyhood, I
> turned to the left with the
> confidence of a little child that
> runs to his mother when he is afraid
> or in distress, to say to Virgil:
> "Not a drop of blood is left in me
> that does not tremble; *I know the*
> *marks of the ancient flame.*"
> (30.34–48; my italics)

As the pilgrim turns for comfort and guidance to Virgil, Virgil has disappeared, yielding his place to Beatrice and leaving the pilgrim in inconsolable tears. At no point in the poem is Virgil's poetry more visible than at this moment when, his role as a character finished, he is replaced by Beatrice and returned to Limbo.

Dante is neither a romantic poet deriving from the loss of Virgil a sense of the irresolvable, nor is he Virgil, embittered by unchangeable tragedy. Beatrice's first words rebuke the pilgrim for his weeping: "Dante, because Virgil leaves thee weep not, weep not yet, for thou must weep for another sword" (30.55–57). We are reminded of Augustine's words of reproach to himself for weeping over Virgil's poetry:

> "*I broke my troth with you* [God] *and*
> embraced another while applause
> echoed about me. For to love this
> world is to break troth with you,
> yet men applaud and are ashamed to
> be otherwise. I did not weep over

this, but instead I wept for Dido,
who surrendered her life to the
sword, while I forsook
you. . . ."

(*Confessions* 1.13)

The "other sword" that Beatrice threatens the pilgrim with is precisely the guilt of having broken faith with her, of having been, like Augustine who gave in to the love of this world, an unfaithful lover. Furthermore, when the pilgrim finally formulates his admission of guilt, it is in the unexpectedly general terms of the deviation toward "present things" (31.34), the things of this world that "turned my steps with their false pleasure as soon as your face was hid" (31.35–36). Infidelity to Beatrice is remarkably like infidelity to God.

Dante's reunion with his lover is a very complicated event, even further from our modern expectations for a love story than are the events of the *Vita Nuova*. Those events are repeatedly recalled in this section of the poem, making it absolutely clear that Dante wishes us to read his journey to Beatrice in the *Divine Comedy* as a continuation, or better, as the fulfillment of his work in the *Vita Nuova*. It is impossible to state simply the radical nature of Dante's use of tradition in this important part of the poem. He writes consistently as a love poet, celebrating a real woman whose hold on him continued even after her death. At the same time, he presents his love theme boldly in theological terms, as a conversion in the Augustinian tradition. The commitment to God that Augustine found after so much searching is the very commitment that Beatrice demands of the pilgrim. Augustine's metaphor of the love of this world as infidelity to the only true object of love has been turned around and become once again literally the betrayal of a lover. Because the pilgrim's love for Beatrice is, at this stage, indistinguishable from his love for Christ, the smallest deviation from it is as abominable as the ones Augustine describes so often in the *Confessions,* such as his weeping over Dido's death. Dante has found a way of putting Beatrice in God's place without falling into the literary idolatry characteristic of those medieval love poets who employed religious images to portray their lovers and exalt them above all other things. He has contrived a new way of celebrating love, a love poetry that is religious not just on the rhetorical level, but in its essence as well. Stated simply, the overpowering feelings the pilgrim has always had for Beatrice are presented as a gift of God's grace, an opening of his soul toward a more transcendent beauty that she already reflected in life and reflects more powerfully now, as she will tell him, after death. She is his particular way to salvation and she will literally lead him to Christ.

And what of Virgil, who is left behind when Beatrice arrives? What of the pilgrim's tears for him? Saint Augustine rejected his own sensitivity to the humanity of Virgil's poetry as part of his misguided attachment to the things of this world. Does Dante too reject Virgil in this sense by leaving him behind when Beatrice arrives? I think the answer is to be found in the voices announcing "eternal life" with the Virgilian words expressing the despair of humanity without that announcement. Although the character Virgil can go no further, nor guide the pilgrim past this point in the journey to salvation, the humanity he so powerfully exemplifies is saved through the God he did not know and whose angels, in an unequaled tribute to him, choose his very words to announce that salvation. Dante and Augustine are close in their understanding of conversion. Indeed Augustine is surely Dante's most important source for his literary "confessions." But for Dante, unlike Augustine, the human wisdom that the character of Virgil portrays, and all that is associated with it, including the pagan society of Rome, is simply insufficient, not evil or dangerous. The beauty of Virgil's poetry does not have to be rejected, for it reflects the truth he did not know, even to the point of furnishing suitable words to announce it. At the very moment the pagan disappears from the poem, his poetry becomes fully integrated into Dante's Christian message.

Eden. At the top of Purgatory Virgil, whose role has been the transitory one of a temporal father (and mother), disappears, leaving the pilgrim under the authority of his lover, who will not guide him with rules but by mediation and inspiration. Once the pilgrim confesses and renounces definitively the smallest infidelity to her, her conversion is complete and his soul ready for the fulfillment toward which all desire tends. Theologically, he has been redeemed, restored to the justice Adam lost. Poetically, he has been reunited to the woman whose brightness has dominated his life from childhood. Symbolically, he has, with the help of Virgil, found and traveled the lost path to the sun that he was searching for in the prologue scene. Geographically, he is on the globe's highest peak, literally on the top of the world. Finally, and perhaps most important, he is in Eden, the place where man was created in innocence and would have lived in natural justice had not the first parents sinned.

Just after they arrive in Eden, before Beatrice's appearance, Virgil dismisses his pupil, proclaiming him free to wander about at will in this place where man was created free. As he wanders he sees a beautiful maiden, Matelda, singing and dancing in joy at the Creator, and is filled with a longing and nostalgic love. This love is clearly the universal desire for lost innocence, the natural need for justice that, in Dante's theology, has not been alienated from man. Fallen man desires his irretrievable original state and, although that innocence can never be regained, its memory, which inspires the pilgrim's nostalgic love for Matelda on his way to Beatrice, is still an integral part of human nature. The remedy to humanity's great loss through Adam is Christ, who reopens Paradise to him. But Christ does not turn time backward or return humanity to Eden; rather, He provides humanity with a new goal, the heavenly Paradise that supplants the earthly one. In a sense very prominent in Christianity, Christ offers man more than he originally had, but Christ does not restore what was man's and was lost by man. And so, while Eden is the place where the pilgrim sheds his guilt and visits the home of human nature, neither he nor any other soul dwells here. The return to Eden is not a return home, but a stop on the way to man's new home.

> Those who in old times sang of the
> age of gold and of its happy state
> perhaps dreamed on Parnassus of this

place; here the human root was
innocent, here was lasting spring
and every fruit, this is the nectar
of which each tells.

(28.139–47)

Dante takes care to draw our attention to the identification of this
place with what the pagans called the Golden Age, the age in which
the world was pure and innocent and in which suffering, pain, and
labor were unknown. That the ancients dreamt of this place on Par-
nassus confirms that, in Dante's interpretation, fallen man has not lost
his natural desire for justice, reflected in the universal nostalgia represented by the ancient poets through the myth of the Golden Age,
and so strongly reawakened in the pilgrim as he gazes on Matelda.

However, there is one important difference between the Golden
Age and the Christian myth of Eden. The Golden Age is represented
as a new beginning that recurs each time the world degenerates to
destruction. It is part of a cosmic cycle analogous to the annual cycle
of the seasons. In the Christian tradition, there is no such repetition.
The world is created only once at the beginning and it will end at
Judgment Day, or at least history will end. Time does not go around
in eternal circles; it begins and ends and has a central event in the
birth, death, and resurrection of Christ. There is no repetition, no return to Eden, no more earthly paradise for man. But, through Christ,
there is a resolution, an end, and a new home for man in the heavenly
paradise.

In Dante's poem, Eden, the place where man began, is also a place
of ending. Justice is restored, Beatrice returns, the pageantry of history
passes before him. He confesses, is judged by Beatrice and taken back
by her. At this point, the pageant and Beatrice combine to reveal an
apocalyptic vision that charges him with the mission of carrying its
message to his readers. The completion of the pilgrim's personal history in his conversion and reunion with Beatrice reflects and is reflected by a vision of the completion of mankind's history. This scene,
where all of the events of time seem to come to a conclusion, would
be the end of the poem if Dante did not believe in a dimension beyond

time. But, like everything else in the *Purgatorio,* the images of universal history point beyond themselves to a transcendent resolution.

The Poetics of the Purgatorio. Before concluding, we would do well to look again at the cosmological side of the poem, or the universe as Dante's central metaphor. At the end of the journey that took the pilgrim down so that he could travel in a cosmically upward direction, we find Eden, the home of natural man. It is the end of his journey to Beatrice and it is the highest point in the world. He has traveled all the way down as far as Satan and now he has traveled all the way up as far as the place of original human innocence. The path to justice through death and regeneration appears retrospectively as a message inscribed in the world itself. Dante has taken the world as his age understood it, that is as a sphere held together by gravity and inhabited only in its lower hemisphere, as the basis of his metaphor. From the beliefs of his traditional faith he has taken the fall of Satan, the Garden of Eden, Hell, and Purgatory and placed them in the physical structure of the world. Where Satan, Eden, Hell, or Purgatory might be was unknown, not determined by the teachings concerning them. By the simple maneuver of locating these four, all of which hypothetically might be where he placed them, he has made the road he traveled appear concrete and objective while still spiritually charged with the central message of his faith. Because the pilgrim is fallen, as all men are, in order to travel toward the justice lost to him, he must aim toward the light of the world. In order to reach it he must travel downward to the point where down becomes up. Then he can travel toward the light to which he was drawn from the beginning. He is guided on a path through the world that reveals the Creator's message in it, which is a reading of an unremittingly concrete text.

The drama of the Fall and redemption has left its mark on the reality Dante represents and the laws of nature cooperate in rendering a message that came after them. Satan's moral weight coincides with the pull the Earth has on all bodies and, conversely, in Purgatory that pull will lessen gradually and disappear. The pilgrim is told early in his journey up the mountain that, while it will be a hard climb at the beginning, by the time he reaches the top his body will be virtually weightless. As a matter of fact, when he and Beatrice leave the mountain for the final stage of the journey, he will find himself accelerating upward, released from the gravity of the earth and pulled by the far greater force of the attraction of God. This upward gravity is not represented as against natural laws but as part of a superior set of natural laws. The soul freed by Purgatory is subjected to a mysterious spiritual gravity that obliterates the far lesser gravity pertaining to man's physical nature.

The downward force of degeneration in Hell and the upward force of regeneration in Purgatory are portrayed as messages written into the physical laws of the created world. In the *Paradiso* we shall see how Dante portrays the universe itself as primarily expressive, but for the moment we should deal with the expressiveness peculiar to Purgatory. While Satan's gravity coincides perfectly with the physical laws governing the world of the four elements, natural physical laws in Purgatory are altered in view of their expressive purpose. The maker of those very laws manipulates them, as only He can, to make everything on the mountain primarily expressive. One episode is particularly significant in this regard.

Just before the travelers meet Statius, the pilgrim is terrified by a great tremor of the mountain. A deathly chill seizes him while a cry goes up from everywhere on the mountain of "*Gloria in excelsis Deo*," or the song announcing the birth of Christ first heard by the shepherds:

> I felt the mountain shake like a
> thing that is falling; at which a
> chill seized me such as seizes one
> that goes to his death. Assuredly
> Delos was not shaken so hard before
> Latona made her nest there to give
> birth to the two eyes of heaven.
> Then began on all sides such a shout
> that the master drew close to me,
> saying: "Do not fear while I guide

thee." "*Gloria in excelsis Deo*"
were the words of all, by what I
made out from those near, where the
cry could be understood. We stood
motionless and in suspense, like the
shepherds who first heard that song,
until it was ended and the trembling
ceased.

(20.127–41)

The earthquake, simultaneously suggesting death and birth, fills the frightened pilgrim with a longing, the greatest he has ever experienced, to understand its mystery. Statius explains the earthquake as part of what he calls the "religion of the mountain" (21.41–42). An ordinary earthquake is the result of physical causes but, from the gates of Purgatory upward, such causes are not effective. Miraculously, when "wind that is hidden in the earth" (21.56) shakes the base of the mountain, the upper part that rests on it does not move. In fact, Purgatory is free from all change due to natural phenomena such as heat, cold, wind, rain, or snow. The earthquake just experienced was of a miraculous nature. The mountain trembled not because the earth below moved, but because a soul was ready to leave its purgatorial penance. Each time this happens, all of the souls in Purgatory share in song the joy of the one who has been freed.

The explanation of the earthquake is much more than a detail of Purgatory, it is a momentous revelation about the nature of this realm. In Purgatory, natural phenomena are above their own laws, obedient only to their expressive purpose. Like miracles, they are supernatural; like human art, they give outward expression to their Maker's intention.

We watch Purgatory's "miracles" throughout the *cantica*: on the island's shore Virgil plucks a rush and it grows back instantaneously; the carvings in the terrace of the proud reveal to the eyes the audible words of their representations; forward motion is not possible without the light of the sun; souls grow thin from desire of food; the pilgrim passes through a wall of fire that burns him physically without scorching so much as a hair on his head. The mountain accomplishes its purpose through the divine art, peculiar to it and to miracles, of superseding the internal laws of nature to express through it the divine presence. Like other art—and nature itself is the model of all art—Purgatory's manipulates the imagination and, through it, desire.

Purgatory, compared to the other two realms, is based on principles of artifice, illusion, manipulation of the imagination, and moral edification. Objective reality is subservient to what seems, what is meant, what is signified. The mountain is the means to climb to the sun. But the sun, the "planet that leads men straight on every road," the light without which a line on the ground cannot be passed, is charged with meaning other than the literal. Manipulation in the *Purgatorio* is characterized by "not false errors" (*Purgatorio* xv.117), illusions that distort outward reality in order to make the message dominant over it. While sin "makes the crooked road seem straight" (10.3), the mountain straightens those "which the world made crooked" (23.126). Working on the imagination, it reverses the damage done through the imagination. Too often in this world the soul is distracted from the divine message by the splendor of its signs. God's art in Purgatory, so like man's, temporarily removes the independent reality of the signs, through illusion and disregard of their inherent laws, and by so doing makes them point unequivocally to their transcendent message. The *Paradiso* will deal more directly with that message.

CHAPTER VI

The *Paradiso*

THE STRUCTURE OF THE *PARADISO*

Dante once said: "The literal sense must come first, for it is the one in whose meaning the others are enclosed and without which it would be impossible and irrational to interpret the others" (*Convivo* 2.1). I sometimes wish that more of Dante's interpreters took to heart this simple principle, especially where the *Paradiso* is concerned. Our reading can only be a distortion unless we start by looking at the *Paradiso* as exactly what it claims to be, a voyage through space, made possible by supernatural means that allowed its protagonist to visit the unreachable stars and experience the inaccessible realms of reality. Since the extraordinary literal level of the *Paradiso* is ultimately also its message, I will preface my discussion with a summary of it.

Still on top of the mountain of Purgatory, the pilgrim watches Beatrice as she turns her eyes on the sun and gazes into its brightness. Almost compelled by her action, he, too, holds his eyes on the sun as long as he can, longer than would normally be possible, and then turns them back to Beatrice's eyes, whereby he is marvelously lifted from Earth and transported at an inconceivable velocity upward to the sky. Beatrice explains that he is being propelled by the attraction of the ultimate goal of all rational creatures, God. Although this upward acceleration in defiance of physical laws might seem to be unnatural, it is actually as truly natural as the downward flow of a stream. Having acquired the freedom to move unimpeded toward the object of all desire, to do otherwise would be no more natural or possible than for a flame to lie down on the ground. Creation is "the great sea of being" through which all things are driven by natural inclination toward the port of their fulfillment. Fire rises, streams flow downward, stones fall, animals behave according to instinct, and it is the pilgrim's newly freed instinct that is causing the rising of his body. Man is uniquely both physical and spiritual, a unity of body and soul. The natural upward inclination of his unity is far stronger than the pull of gravity to which his body is subjected. This instinct is carrying the pilgrim through the heavens toward his goal and their source.

In medieval cosmology there were nine heavens, or spheres, revolving around the still Earth. These spheres were transparent and circled in a regular pattern around the world of the four elements. The first carried the moon with it, the fourth the sun, the eighth the stars called "fixed stars" because their positions relative to each other remained constant—and the others except for the ninth each carried a planet. While other aspects of the trajectories observed in the sky were accounted for by more complicated theories, the rising and setting of the celestial bodies was explained by the theory of the spheres. The ninth sphere, called the *Primum Mobile* because it was considered to be the first moving part and the origin of motion in space, carried no bodies in its revolution but contained all the rest. This mysterious, invisible heaven was the edge of space. The nine spheres were thought to be turned by angels who, spiritually moved by their love of God, transmitted that love to the spheres as physical motion.

By looking at Beatrice the pilgrim is lifted from one to the other of all nine heavens and, as they rise, Beatrice's eyes become brighter and his own stronger. In each sphere he encounters souls, as he had done in the circles of Hell and on the terraces of Purgatory, and he learns from them of truths and mysteries he had not been able to understand or to know on Earth. Different from the souls he met previously, these are not shades, images of their former bodies, but spiritual presences bright with the love and joy they feel. They express concepts verbally, but feelings by glowing, twirling, singing, and positioning themselves collectively in shapes symbolic of great mysteries or intangible graces. Their expressiveness is modeled in many of its details on the regular motions of the heavenly bodies with which they work in harmony. Unlike these bodies, however, the positions of the souls in the sky are not permanent. They visit the various parts of the universe's structure in order to clarify for the pilgrim both its message and theirs. Their true dwelling place is beyond space where the pilgrim will see them again, at the end of his journey, congregated around God in positions reflected by the temporary ones they assumed in the spatial order of the universe.

Their real home, the Empyrean, is the last place visited by the pilgrim and can be called a place only metaphorically, for it is outside of space, beyond the *Primum Mobile*. It is the spiritual realm of God, where the blessed and the angels dwell in a harmony centered on and derived from God and reflected in the order of the universe. Of this realm Dante can speak only metaphorically, borrowing his terms from those of physical reality, but the metaphor is a paradoxical one. Everything that is said through it is both true and not true at the same time. For example, the Empyrean is metaphorically outside of space, but to speak more truly, space is an extension of it. Metaphorically, the Empyrean is nowhere, for it is beyond space, but in a truer sense it is space that is excluded from it. "There near and far neither add nor take away" (30.121). Distance and closeness are paradoxically not measured by the space between things. In truth, inside, outside, near, far, beyond, around do not apply to this realm, but since our experience and our language furnish us with no other terms with which to describe the Empyrean, the description must be pure metaphor.

In this realm of pure light, Beatrice leaves the pilgrim's side to take her place among the souls congregated in adoration. She smiles one last time at the pilgrim and, her mediating mission completed, returns her gaze to God. For her lover's salvation, she has "left [her] footprints in hell" and "drawn [him] from bondage into liberty" (31.81, 85). Now she relinquishes her role to the great mystic, Saint

Bernard, who prays to Mary that she intercede with her Son so that the pilgrim may be granted the final vision of the face of God. As he looks into God's face, he first sees all other things as they were conceived prior to their independent being and then he sees the great mysteries of God's own nature, the Trinity and the Incarnation. The vision of the Incarnation, however, so overpowers him that his story and the poem end, but not before one final *terzina* to describe himself as caught up on the motion of "the love that moves the sun and the other stars."

Poetry Versus Theology. Even from so brief a description of the *Paradiso*'s voyage, it is clear that Dante is dealing with ideas that are not only culturally remote from us moderns, but philosophically difficult even for his earlier audiences. Near the beginning of the *Paradiso*, he himself warns us that to follow his poetry we will need an exceptional intellectual background:

> O ye who in a little bark, eager to
> listen, have followed behind my ship
> that singing makes her way, turn
> back to see your shores again; do
> not put forth on the deep, for,
> perhaps, losing me, you would be
> left bewildered.
>
> (2.1–6)

The demands this *cantica* places on its reader's intellectual preparation are no doubt the reason it is relatively much less widely read and appreciated than the *Inferno*. In my opinion, however, far from being the heavy doctrinal work it is often alleged to be, the *Paradiso* is the crowning glory of the *Divine Comedy*. But to appreciate it we must approach its poetry as a conceptualization that has become a vision. We must distinguish between ideas and ideas transformed into images. The object of the *Paradiso* is no more the presentation of doctrine than its fiction is theologically orthodox. What we have here is far less theology, or philosophy, or doctrine of any kind than it is Beatrice's smile opening the universe's mysteries to her faithful lover, disembodied souls shining with love, spiritual twirling, singing, and dancing in harmony with the bright spinning heavens, the overpowering of the soul by God. The *Paradiso*'s poetry is disciplined, intellectually powerful, deeply thoughtful, and rational, but it is ultimately the poetry of pure vision, entirely imagined, entirely devoted to expression.

While the thought the *Paradiso* contains is sophisticated by any standards, the poetry that emerges from it is, in its way, surprisingly simple. The *Paradiso* was not written as a treatise and should not be read as one. Whatever we learn of the intellectual background of Dante's weighty speculation enhances our appreciation of his poetry, but is not an end in itself. It is a way to understand Dante's mind so that we can better share his vision. Let me illustrate my point with an extreme but typical example.

Paradiso 2 has the reputation of being so burdened by technical problems arising from medieval debates on the moon spots as to be hardly worth the modern reader's attention. However, even a superficial reading will reveal that, as a matter of fact, the pilgrim's questions about the dark areas of the moon trigger a far broader discussion of the nature of everything that appears in the skies. In simplified philosophical terms, Beatrice is teaching the pilgrim to stress, in his observation of the celestial spectacle, qualitative, not just quantitative differences. The moon is not the same all over for the same reason that each star is different from all the rest, qualitatively different, not just larger or smaller or dimmer or brighter. That reason is ultimately in the Creator, who is all things in one, but whose variety is differentiated in His Creation. With no more information than this we are prepared to read the poetry of Beatrice lovingly revealing to her friend the truth of seeing in the multitude of sparkling stars, not just the size and quantity of what has been created, but the almost infinite variety of it.

Let us look at a few lines:

> . . . the heaven that so many lights
> make fair takes its stamp from the
> profound mind that turns it, and of
> that stamp becomes itself the seal;

and as the soul within your dust is
diffused through different members
that are adapted to various
faculties, so the Intelligence
unfolds its bounty, multiplied
through the stars, itself wheeling
on its own unity. Diverse virtue
makes diverse alloy with the
precious body which it quickens and
with which, even as life in you, it
is bound; by the joyous nature
whence it springs the mingled virtue
shines through the body as joy
through the living pupil.

(2.130–44)

While concepts, difficult concepts, are presented in this passage, the language, dominated by images, is concrete and even simple. Beatrice's words are less a statement of doctrine than an expression of insight. She is opening the pilgrim's mind to the vision of the universe's message. The Creator's mind, "wheeling on its own unity," gives a multiple illustration of all the goodness it contains through the variety of the created stars. Beatrice's comparison of Creation to the mysterious power that gives life to "the dust of our bodies," is both simple and powerful. Were it a philosophical assertion of a theory of an animated universe, which it is not in any sense, it would be ordinary at best. But it expresses a poetic, not a technical, comparison, intended to awaken our sensitivity both to the significant nature of the stars' beauty and the mystery of animation in the human body. The analogy between creation and life lies in the incomprehensible relation of the intangible to the tangible, illustrated in different ways by both. "By the joyous nature from whence it springs the mingled virtue shines through the body [of the stars] as joy through the living pupil." Sparkling stars and smiling eyes could hardly be more familiar sights, more concrete images. But as Beatrice speaks to the pilgrim she evokes in him, by the comparison between them, a new sense both of the message in the stars and of the mystery in the ability of the physical eye to communicate the emotions of the soul; "through the *living* pupil," for there is nothing in the eye itself, an inanimate thing, that can explain its expressive power. Beatrice does, here and elsewhere, make technical points and introduce statements of doctrine, but they function as parts of a whole, as a means to the end of offering the pilgrim not just intellectual answers but a vision and an experience of the truth. The poet himself best describes the effect Beatrice's so-called technical discussion produces: "That sun which first warmed my breast with love had discovered to me, by proof and refutation, fair truth's sweet aspect" (3.1–3).

By underscoring a direct appeal to the imagination in a passage commonly considered tormented by abstractions, I am not suggesting that the *Paradiso* is simple or easy to understand and far less that we read it impressionistically. I am saying, however, and this will be the underlying theme of my entire discussion, that the *Paradiso* is not only expressive in nature, but is also about expression. In emphasizing this point, I am, of course, trying to steer my reader away from commonly held prejudices that confuse the great learning that prepared Dante to write the last *cantica* with the poetic creation he produced. Finally, I am trying to convince my reader of the timeless rewards in store for his efforts to understand the depth and complexity of the most frequently misunderstood and misrepresented part of the poem. To help him along the way I will try to clarify some of the ideas that seem most important to me for a good reading of this work in which, more than in any other, thought and imagination seem indistinguishable.

Transcendence. The *Purgatorio* exhausts the story of the human voyage, leaving the poet with the exceptional task of recapturing in his memory images of the "transhuman" level of the pilgrim's experience and representing them to his readers. "The passing beyond humanity could not be set forth in words; let the example suffice, therefore, for him to whom grace reserves the experience" (1.70–72). "The passing beyond humanity" translates the Italian *"trasumanare,"* a verb coined by Dante to define his subject as not only beyond our language but beyond our experience as well. In this important statement Dante both denies and affirms the poetic feasibility of his representation. The experience is not ours now, but it is reserved for us by grace—after death. Language is not adaptable to it and yet we are reading words about it.

The lines that follow this important statement contain an equally important allusion to Saint Paul: "If I was only that part of me which Thou createdst last, Thou knowest, Love that rulest the heavens, who with Thy light didst raise me" (1.73–75). Although Dante expresses uncertainty about whether his voyage was taken only in the spirit (the part of man created last is the soul), the point is not to place any doubt on the presence throughout of the pilgrim's body, but rather to recall to his readers the familiar words of Saint Paul: "I know a man in Christ . . . whether in the body or out of the body I do not know, God knows—that he was caught up into Paradise and heard secret words that man may not repeat" (2 Cor. 12:2). Saint Paul's claim to have been caught up into Paradise was widely understood in the Middle Ages as the claim to have had a total vision of God. It was to this passage that Dante alluded early in the *Inferno* when the pilgrim hesitated to follow Virgil because "I am not Aeneas, I am not Paul" (*Inferno* 2.31). He spoke then of Aeneas's voyage to the underworld and Saint Paul's vision of heaven as exceptional allowances because of the roles they were to play in providential history: the one making the Roman Empire possible, the other spreading Christianity within it. Dante's Pauline words at the beginning of the *Paradiso* not only suggest that his pilgrim is far more like Aeneas and Paul than he thought, but they also have further implications. Saint Paul, in stating that he had a vision, declined to express it, for it is impossible for man to speak of such things. Dante, too, points out the ineffability of his subject—"the passing beyond humanity could not be set forth in words"—but the ineffability, which should preclude his poetics, is stated rather as part of them, as an element to be kept in mind by the reader: "let the example suffice, therefore."

In a general sense, the example must always suffice, for all language is metaphorical and all communication is indirect. That is to say, language cannot pass the experiences, the intangible feelings, and the responses of one person to another. But, through its conventions, language refers to common experiences, thereby making it possible to share personal experiences in the limited way we call communication. Here, however, Dante refers to a problem beyond the general limitation of all language, a problem specific to his task in this part of the poem. The experience he will speak of—and unlike Saint Paul he *will* speak of it—is supernatural, "transhuman," and therefore the terms of conventional language derived from experience are incompatible with it. Words designed to reflect human experience must somehow invent new meaning for themselves in order to express things beyond human experience.

Dante's important statement about his poetics leads to subtle theoretical questions, but it also leads to more simple considerations, ones more useful in the present context. What is the literal sense of "trasumanare"? In what specific ways is the pilgrim's experience beyond ours? First, his senses, particularly his sight, are transformed so that not only can he tolerate ever greater brightness without being blinded, but also, as we shall discover, he can perceive things that are spiritual and therefore invisible. Second, he visits in the flesh unreachable parts of the universe, places we can only view from immeasurable distances and toward which we can only stretch our imagination. Third, and least obvious, his experience is beyond time, at least in the human sense of the sequence of events that constitute a life or a period or history itself. This might well be missed because, in retelling the experience, the poet has organized the voyage sequentially for the reader's benefit. But, when it is missed, the message of some of the most important episodes in the *Paradiso* is also lost.

THE TRANSCENDENCE OF HISTORY

At the end of the *Purgatorio* the return to Eden, the procession of history, the reunion with Beatrice, the apocalyptic visions all combine to suggest the completion of history, the end of the story's temporal development. The *Purgatorio* is strewn with references to the hour of the day, the position of the sun, the amount of time spent in one or the other place, the arrival of evening, the beginning of a new day, references that indirectly remind the reader of the shortness and unpredictability of his mortal life and the urgency of correcting it. But when time is mentioned in the *Paradiso*, it is in paradoxical terms that deny rather than affirm its passing. Typically, the pilgrim is swept from heaven to inconceivably distant heaven at such velocity that he seems to arrive before he departs. Whatever time is in the paradisial experience, it transcends what we measure in hours or days or years.

Historical time is the flowing of events from their beginning to their end. For humanity it flows from Eden to Judgment Day, for each man from birth to death. Time is marked by change, which does not exist outside of its dimension, and consequently by imperfection and anxiety. All generation and corruption, all change, occur beneath the sphere of the moon, which divides the world of temporality from the immortal heavens that, themselves unchanging, measure time and frame change with their even turning. It is not clear whether in the fiction any hours or days actually pass while the pilgrim is in the heavens, but it is certain that the unchanging realm he visits transcends history. Our interpretation of important parts of the *Paradiso* often depends on keeping this in mind. In fact, many episodes seem to deal with worldly topics and many common misreadings of them stem from the assumption that the manner of dealing with them is also worldly. This, in my opinion, is never true.

Historical and political subjects are consistently interpreted from outside the frame of their temporal dimension. We might, for instance, consider the souls in the heaven of the sun who present themselves in a kind of astronomical dance around the pilgrim. The conversation with these souls, who are great Church thinkers and writers, revolves around the subject of the idealistic origin and present corruption of the sometimes rival orders, the Franciscans and the Dominicans. Among the twenty-four souls who turn about the pilgrim and Beatrice are also representatives of conflicting schools of theology. Great Church leaders are honored, but corruption in the religious orders is deplored and problems and conflicts in the official Church's daily work of teaching and spreading doctrine are suggested. Much that is imperfect on Earth is represented here and the criticism of those imperfections might seem to be the subject of the episode. But, even under moderate observation, not conflict but its resolution is portrayed. Beyond earthly differences, the Dominican Thomas and the Franciscan Bonaventura each make a point of celebrating the other's order and of deploring the corruption and disgrace of his own. The message this group of souls brings to the pilgrim is one of harmony beyond the Earth, as they evoke over and over the perfectly ordered motions of the heavenly bodies whose different courses work smoothly together to form one splendid pattern.

Differences on Earth inevitably produce conflict. One goal interferes with another; if one theologian is right, then another who disagrees must be wrong; even good intentions can be obstructed by man's imperfections. But over all the disorder and conflict of earthly goings-on presides the protective force of Providence, sending to its Church, in moments of need, such men as Saint Francis and Saint Dominic. The resolution of conflict in the perfect harmony of the heavens, which dominates the imagery throughout the episode, serves to illustrate the providential order that presides from outside time over the events of time. The transcendent resolution of conflict and the perspective it gives to the limited conditions of existence within time constitute the message of these beautiful cantos. The pilgrim's experience of detachment from worldly events echoes in the poet's words of admonishment:

> O insensate care of mortals, how
> vain are the reasonings that make
> thee beat thy wings in downward
> flight! One was going after law,
> another after the *Aphorisms*, one
> following the priesthood and another
> seeking to rule by force or craft,
> one set on robbery and another on
> affairs of state, one labouring in
> the toils of fleshly delights and

another given up to idleness; while
I, set free from all things, was
high in heaven with Beatrice,
received thus gloriously.

(11.1–12)

Another brief example of the supernatural treatment Dante gives
to an apparently political subject occurs in the heaven of Jupiter. In
this sphere the pilgrim encounters the just rulers of the Earth, who
arrange their luminous spirits in letter after letter until they have written a message of justice on Earth across the sky. Then they form the
shape of a lily and finally that of an eagle, the imperial sign of justice.
This passage is usually cited as a political representation of order in
which the many—the souls, standing for the citizens—make up the
parts of the one—the Eagle, standing for the Empire. The functioning
of the many in view of the common goal did indeed dominate Dante's
political ideology and it is true that, in its way, the Eagle does celebrate
this ideal. But the key word here is "ideal." What the pilgrim sees
could never be imagined on Earth, let alone accomplished.

And that of which I have now to tell
never tongue conveyed, nor ink
wrote, nor ever was conceived by
fancy. For I saw and I heard the
beak talk and utter with its voice *I*
and *mine* when its meaning was *we* and
ours.

(19.7–12)

His vision, in fact, is of many spirits filled with justice, forming not
the parts of something else in the artificial sense that the citizens are
parts of the body politic, but a mysteriously organic being that speaks
with one voice moving up through the throat and coming out of the
beak. This being is a congregation of many souls, but still incomprehensibly singular. It is Justice itself, that which is the same in every
just action, that of which every just action is an example, or a partial

and indirect manifestation. What the pilgrim sees is both real, because the souls are real, and unimaginable, because justice cannot be envisaged as an essence separate from its manifestations. The single-voiced chorus of this miraculously formed being speaks of order in this world only briefly and remotely. Its message, and the subject of its lengthy speech, is the unfathomable mystery of Providence or the divine justice that transcends human history.

Cacciaguida. The central episode in the *Paradiso*, spanning three cantos, occurs in the heaven of Mars, where the pilgrim's ancestor, Cacciaguida, enlightens him on many things, and especially on the future in store for him after his return to Earth. The meeting of the two is intended to recall that of Aeneas with his father in the underworld, during which Anchises reveals Aeneas's momentous destiny to him and inspires him with the strength to fulfill it. And just so, it is from Cacciaguida that the pilgrim, along with the reader, gets a clear statement of the providential nature of the voyage and the poetic mission it entails. No episode in the *Paradiso* is more directly concerned with this life or more frequently distorted by interpretations that fail to recognize that the temporal issues are dealt with in terms of their resolution outside of time. Unfortunately, because few episodes are as complex as this one, my treatment of it will be especially incomplete, using it primarily as an example of Dante's representation of the perspective beyond time.

After a long conversation between the pilgrim and his ancestor about the early, pure days of their common city, Florence, and about its present corruption, the discussion turns to the future. The pilgrim is apprehensive because he has heard—from Ciacco, Farinata, Brunetto Latini, and others—predictions about his life, particularly his political life. He is also concerned about repeating to the world those parts of his vision that could be unwelcome to the powerful. Cacciaguida's answers to the pilgrim are commonly taken as powerful revelations of Dante's bitterness over events that had already taken place as he wrote the poem, but that had not yet occurred in the fictional year of the pilgrim's voyage. In other words—in the common view—

Dante takes this opportunity of a fictional prophecy to lament the injustice of his exile and to express his bitterness over the indignities and hardships it imposed on him. The prophecy, we are told, brings our attention back to Earth, revealing the most human side of Dante, his anger at the corruption of which he was a victim and his painful nostalgia for his home.

I believe Dante would have been horrified at such an interpretation of this important episode, whose point is precisely to transcend this kind of limited perspective. Like Anchises's on which it is modeled, Cacciaguida's message is, after all, clearly one of ultimate triumph. It presents good news, although not in the sense that what the pilgrim fears—injustice, exile, poverty, separation from family and home, humiliation, degradation—will not happen and will not be painful. His worst fears will in fact come true, but, beyond the limited suffering these misfortunes will cause him, beyond anything that will happen during his years on Earth, his soul and his poem will triumph. Let me just cite a few of the more triumphant phrases ignored by those who see this passage as a document of frustration and sadness: "As sweet harmony comes . . . to the ear, comes to my sight the time that is in store for thee" (17.43–45); "the vengeance shall be testimony to the truth that dispenses it" (17.53–54); "they, not thou, shall have the brows red for this" (17.66); "it shall be to thine honour to have made a party by thyself" (17.68–69); "thy life shall far outlast the punishment of their perfidies" (17.98–99); "if thy voice is grievous at first taste, it will afterwards leave vital nourishment" (17.130–31); "This cry of thine shall do as does the wind, which strikes most on the highest summits; and that is no small ground of honour" (17.133–135).

Cacciaguida is not just telling his descendant that the long-term outlook is better than the short-term one. He is explicitly revealing the pilgrim's life as it is definitively understood from outside of time, in the unchanging and infallible mind of God:

> Contingency, which does not extend
> beyond the volume of your material
> world, is all depicted in the
> Eternal Vision, yet does not thence

derive necessity, any more than does
a ship that drops down stream from
the eyes in which it is mirrored;
from thence, as sweet harmony comes
from an organ to the ear, comes to
my sight the time that is in store
for thee.

(17.37–45)

Contingency, by definition that which may or may not occur, is peculiar to time and by its very nature uncertain. We live on Earth without knowing what will happen to us or outside of us. This situation produces anxiety in human lives and makes judgment impossible as well. In fact, not only do we not know what will happen, we would not be able to pick wisely what should happen, for we could not know fully the consequences it would bring. As long as time unfolds, the meaning of things can change. I may regret tomorrow what I was thankful for today. And then again, I may be thankful for it once more the next day. In Dante's view, neither an individual life nor events concerning a collectivity can be subjected to certain judgment or true interpretation as long as we live in time.

The sense of the Christian's relation to Providence is precisely in the faith he places in God to watch over all events and assure their final just outcome, for the good Christian trusts only God's judgment, not his own. Cacciaguida's images of the book of our experience ("the *volume* of your material world") and of the painting of it in God's mind ("all *depicted* in the Eternal Vision") stress the contrast between the gradual unfolding, or turning of pages, within time and the complete picture of eternity. These images suggest that Cacciaguida's prophecy is an interpretation and definitive judgment, not just a source of factual information. The hardships endured are obviously not Cacciaguida's message to the pilgrim. The message is rather an illustration of the mysterious words the pilgrim heard as he entered the heaven of Mars: "Arise and conquer" (14.125). His future losses and suffering are part of a picture that reflects the central Christian message of death and resurrection that governs Dante's poem.

Having expressed the eternal truth he has read into the pilgrim's temporal existence, Cacciaguida charges him with the poetic mission of writing the *Divine Comedy*:

> But none the less put away every
> falsehood and make plain all thy
> vision, . . .
>
> . . . .
>
> For that reason have been shown to
> thee, in these wheels, on the
> mountain, and in the woeful valley,
> only souls that are known to fame;
> because the mind of one who hears
> will not pause or fix its faith for
> an example that has its roots
> unknown or hidden or for other proof
> that is not manifest.
>
> (17.127–28, 136–42)

We cannot overstate how revealing these lines are as the conclusion of the encounter with Cacciaguida. This is Dante's clearest and most explicit statement that he believes his poem is a mission. Like Aeneas's and Saint Paul's his exceptional vision was not intended for him alone but for mankind. Had the purpose of this journey been only to show the pilgrim the inalterable truth, he might have encountered friends and neighbors along the way. But, because it was intended to be made public, his encounters are all with souls of well-known people. The examples were chosen to be meaningful not just to Dante but to his readers, and not just to readers of his day but also to those "who will call these times ancient" (17.120).

Providence. Throughout these episodes, time is represented as the dimension in which man lives his mortal life and in which events and things come and go. Man's vision is limited by it and his death assured by it. In the Christian medieval view, historical time is the linear flowing of events from beginning to end. Until the end has been reached, until the story is finished, it is impossible to understand the meaning of these events. Conversely, eternity transcends the dimensions of time, all things being present to it at once. God's eternal knowledge contains all the beginnings and endings, all the causes and results in one picture. Nothing can be changed or reinterpreted. And God, who alone knows what is truly beneficial and what is truly harmful, presides over events in time benevolently, not impeding man's freedom but guaranteeing ultimate justice and ordering all things toward His own good end. The order that God imposes on history is called Providence and is mysterious to man who, from his limited perspective, cannot always see the purpose of apparent evils inflicted on him or interpret the justice of the wicked going unpunished while the innocent suffer.

No writer spoke more poignantly of these matters than Boethius, one of Dante's main sources and a man whose life had extraordinary affinities to Dante's. Like Dante, Boethius was a scientist, a philosopher, a poet, and a popularizer; like Dante, he held high political office; and, like Dante, he was the victim of corruption and false accusations that led to his permanent exile. But this distinguished citizen was treated even more brutally than Dante: Boethius was imprisoned in his exile and finally executed. While in prison, he wrote his most famous work, *The Consolation of Philosophy,* in which he tells how he came to terms with his misfortunes by realizing that we call things fortunate or unfortunate out of ignorance. We think we know what is good or bad, what should or should not happen, while we have no such knowledge at all. Ultimately, Boethius came to see his imprisonment as a good for him, bringing him to the realization that his soul and mind could not be confined and thereby giving him a previously unknown freedom. The belief Boethius stresses over and over is that a great order presides over events, a harmony that transcends them and cannot be comprehended by us.

Dante echoes Boethius throughout the *Divine Comedy,* but most of all in the Cacciaguida episode where he speaks of the troubles of his all too similar life. His intention, however, is no more to lament his own hardships than Boethius's was. Dante dramatizes our point of view with the pilgrim's anxiety and the serene resolution of it with Cacciaguida's access to the providential mind of God. Cacciaguida joyously reads the pilgrim a message of rebirth and Christian triumph in his earthly troubles, showing them to him as reflections of the un-limited providentiality of the Crucifixion and Resurrection of Christ. It is ironic that the very episode where Dante seeks to imagine the confirming of a human life, the answering of its questions, should so often have been read as a representation of unresolved grief. Provi-dence, the transcendent ordering of history reflected in the privileged account of scripture, is the source of Cacciaguida's prophecy and a dominating theme of Dante's poem. It is present from the first canto, where Virgil is sent to save the pilgrim, and its mysterious nature is celebrated by all the Paradisial episodes concerning temporality. But with Cacciaguida, Dante invokes it also as the source of his poetic mission.

THE LETTER AND THE SPIRIT:
THE MYSTERY OF EXPRESSION

Spiritual Reality and The Transcendence of The Senses. Ear-lier, I defined the pilgrim's supernatural experience as beyond the Earth, beyond the senses, and beyond history, artificially dividing his transcendence in view of clarifying my points about the exceptional nature of the *Paradiso*. I have already discussed how the transcendent perspective of Providence dwarfs its obscure reflection in the unfolding events of time and I will soon discuss how the universe also carries the message of the order God's serene nature imposes on all things. But first let us look at the pilgrim's supersensual experience of invisible spiritual reality and the important and paradoxical implications this experience has for the poetics of the *Paradiso*.

The model for the pilgrim's experience in the heavens and the Empyrean is, as we have seen, Saint Paul's rapture and vision of Par-adise. The most influential interpretation of Saint Paul's claim was offered to the Middle Ages by Saint Augustine, who discussed it in several of his works. Saint Augustine understood the Pauline vision to correspond to the one alluded to by Saint Paul himself in an even more famous passage, where he wrote that, while our vision now is dark, like images in a mirror, after death we will see clearly, "face to face" (1 Cor. 13:12). Saint Augustine understood Saint Paul's rapture as the granting to him, before death, of the vision of God face to face. Any vision of God would be extraordinary, to say the least, but Saint Augustine specifically interpreted this vision as dissociated from the senses and formulated an important analysis of human perception around it. Saint Augustine's discussion implies that our direct experience comes to us through the senses and, what we do not experience directly, we imagine as if we had experienced it through the senses. That is to say, we imagine that what we do not see has physical attributes such as shape and color. Spiritual things—angels, God, and, insofar as it can be separated from the body, the human soul—have no shape or color or texture or temperature or size. But we cannot imagine them this way and so, in our minds, we give images to what does not have an image. We think of God with a human shape, we think of angels as having wings. This is because we do not see them "face to face," as we would in the direct spiritual experience that Saint Augustine calls "intellectual vision."

That Saint Augustine relied so heavily on the Pauline expression "face to face" is itself significant, for what he meant is the denial of this phrase's literal and physical meaning. The necessity of metaphor—here, the face—is inherent in the nature of our experience, which is never spiritually direct. For instance, we perceive each other's actions, words, and gestures, but we can only imagine what we conceive to be behind those outward appearances, what the Middle Ages called the soul. When we speak of invisible things that we somehow "sense," we do it either abstractly and generally through terms like "angry," "happy," "unhappy," "good," "bad," or, more specifically and descriptively, through metaphors taken from the world of sense experience. We probably do not realize how often we speak of intangibles, especially internal feelings, in physical and spatial terms. We are "moved," "elated," "uplifted," "dejected," "depressed," "distant," "unsettled," even "torn up" or "thrown off our feet." Saint Augustine interpreted Saint Paul's experience as occurring unmediated by the senses, as it would be, for instance, if we could see another person directly in his feelings, without relying on intuitions produced by the outward expressions of his face or his body or his actions or his voice. Not really "face to face" then, but "soul to soul." In the case of Saint Paul, the vision consisted of God Himself, and this is also Dante's ultimate claim. But, in the meantime, he paradoxically represents the pilgrim's encounters with the souls as an equally direct and spiritual vision of their inward joy and love; the pilgrim sees with his eyes invisible spiritual presences.

The Metaphor of Light. The way Dante expresses the humanly impossible direct insight of spiritual reality is through the image of light. In medieval and classical philosophy, the incorporeal nature of light was an important theme. Light, having no shape, no color, no consistency, no taste or smell, seemed to be virtually immaterial. And yet, it was spread out in space and visible, although not as an object, but as the source of visibility itself. Philosophically, light hovered somewhere between materiality and immateriality, illustrating being and spirituality and giving almost literal meaning to the metaphor of "vision" as ultimate knowledge. In this philosophical context the sun, as the greatest source of light in the physical universe, could only be thought of as expressing divinity to the world of the senses, and so from ancient times it had this meaning.

While the souls in the *Purgatorio* were represented as visible but unsubstantial, those of the *Paradiso* appear invisible but substantial, a feat the poet accomplishes through the image of light and its metaphysical associations. The souls are, in fact, beings made of light, luminous expressions of themselves. The first to appear bear the slightest, virtually imperceivable human features, the almost invisible outlines of faces:

> As through smooth and transparent
> glass, or through limpid and still
> water not so deep that the bottom is
> lost, the outlines of our faces
> return so faint that a pearl on a

> white brow does not come less
> quickly to our eyes, many such faces
> I saw eager to speak.
>
> (3.10–17)

Because they do not appear to be material, the pilgrim mistakenly thinks that they are reflections until Beatrice tells him that, although immaterial, they are indeed real: "these are real beings that thou seest" (3.29). The most tenuous suggestion of eyes and a smile is described in the next heaven, that of Mercury, as the pilgrim meets the great soul of Justinian. Here, it is even clearer that, whatever suggestion óf the human form is expressed by the poet, it is in view of simultaneously obliterating it and replacing it with luminous spiritual energy.

> "I see well how thou nestest in
> thine own light, and that thou
> drawest it from thine eyes, since it
> sparkles whenever thou smilest" . . .
> . . . .
> I said this, directing myself to the
> radiance that had first spoken to
> me, and it then became far brighter
> than before. Like the sun, which
> itself conceals itself by excess of
> light when the heat has gnawed away
> the dense tempering vapours, so with
> increase of happiness the holy form
> hid itself from me within its own
> beams and thus all enclosed answered
> me. . . .
>
> (5.125–28, 130–38)

The outward means of expression disappears in the act of expression itself as the soul hides, "nests," in the emotion of its own smile.

After Mercury, no more even slight reference to the souls' faces appears in the description. Their brightness increases, however, and, along with it, their expressive power. Ablaze with their vision, they manifest not just their joy but stronger and stronger messages of mysterious truth, expressing, often collectively, meaning beyond human understanding. We need only think of the souls in the heaven of Mars who, arranged in the form of the cross, offer the pilgrim much more than the sign they have formed:

> Here my memory defeats my skill, for
> that cross flamed forth Christ so
> that I can find for it no fit
> comparison; but he that takes up his
> cross and follows Christ shall yet
> forgive me for what I leave untold,
> when he sees Christ flash in that
> dawn. ·
>
> (14.103–8)

We might also remember the message of divine justice so mysteriously expressed by the Eagle. As the pilgrim ascends the material universe, both Beatrice and the luminous spirits he encounters are increasingly charged with the intensity of their spiritual message and the pilgrim's human eyes become progressively stronger to withstand the power of the ever greater light that emanates directly from their vision.

The role played by light in the *Paradiso* is central to its paradoxical poetics of simultaneously affirming the expression and denying the outward image of what is intangible and spiritual. Dante claims to have seen with his physical eyes invisible things ranging from the joy of the souls to the essence of justice to the mind of God. His key image is the one that centuries had understood as a symbol divinely created into nature, as the natural metaphor for being, spirituality, and divinity. But, while tradition furnished Dante with the logic of his metaphor, it took his own powerful imagination to turn the philosophical abstraction into a multiform poetic vision of truth projected through love and of answers written in the bright and distant heavens.

The key to appreciating much of the *Paradiso*'s poetry is in understanding that Beatrice and the souls do more than increase the pilgrim's intellectual knowledge; they also fulfill his natural quest for truth as they express their vision of it in God. The luminous expressiveness of the vision the souls joyously share with the pilgrim, enhanced by music and motion, fills him with what we might call spiritual pleasure: pleasure in that it is communicated to him through the senses, spiritual in that it fulfills the desire of his soul. The souls, and especially Beatrice, smile the truth at him, not with eyes or a mouth, but incomprehensibly with the light of their internal vision. In the *Paradiso* Dante seems never to tire of the image of the smile, for it represents the essence of human expressiveness, or the power to project outwardly what is felt inwardly. Above all, Beatrice's smile, the last thing the pilgrim sees of her, is celebrated in its ever more ineffably beautiful splendor, guiding him as a lover and challenging him as an artist. Her supreme role in his poetry is summed up when he attempts to describe her smile as she leads him out of the physical universe into the Empyrean:

> If all that is said of her up to
> this were gathered in one meed of
> praise, it would be little to serve
> this turn; the beauty I saw not only
> surpasses our measures, but I surely
> believe that only its Maker has all
> the joy of it. I own myself beaten
> at this pass more than ever comic or
> tragic poet was baffled by a point
> in his theme; for, like the sun in
> the most wavering sight, the
> remembrance of the sweet smile
> deprives my mind of its very self.
> From the first day I saw her face in
> this life until this sight the
> pursuit in my song has not been cut
> off; but now must my pursuit cease
> from following longer after her
> beauty in my verse, as with every
> artist at his limit.
>
> (30.16–33)

The Universe as Expression. The souls and Beatrice are expressive centers of energy, living messages that present themselves to the pilgrim in a context that, unlike their presence, is neither spiritual nor temporary. This context is the universe itself, penetrated by and shining forth "the glory of Him who moves all things" (1.1). It stretches out before our eyes but far beyond our grasp, as an immense and brilliant spectacle of peaceful harmonious motion. Its order reflects the divine nature that created it: "All things whatsoever have order among themselves, and this is the form that makes the universe resemble God" (1.103–5). For the pilgrim's benefit, the souls descend from their true home beyond space and present themselves in this or that part of the universe's great structure, as a demonstration by analogy of their various positions in the order of the Empyrean. There, the order they observe is not in a spatial structure but in a spiritual harmony among them, as each finds peace in his own way in relation to God. Since the "pattern" of their collective joy can only be presented to the human mind in spatial terms, they use the universe as a frame for their demonstration. They present themselves to the pilgrim in a specific sphere, "not that this sphere is allotted to them, but in sign of the spiritual one" (4.37–38) where they find peace in the place God wills for them. As Beatrice explains:

> It is necessary to speak thus to
> your faculty, since only from sense
> perception does it grasp that which
> it then makes fit for the intellect.
> For this reason Scripture
> condescends to your capacity and
> attributes hands and feet to God,
> having another meaning, and Holy
> Church represents to you with human
> aspect Gabriel and Michael and the
> other who made Tobit whole again.
> (4.40–48)

The physical structure of the universe is a uniquely apt analogy for the spiritual positioning of the souls around God, for the order that governs them is the same. That order is the mark of the Creator, governing the spiritual beatitude of the souls and regulating the spatial motion of the spheres and the temporal events of history. The *Paradiso* is not just about the universe, it is about the universe as God's art in space, or physical reality as the divine language or outward expression of the Creator. The universe is the letter par excellence and the spiritual appearance of the souls in it dramatizes the essence of allegory: the presence, paradoxically literal in this instance, of the spirit in the letter.

But, before and after the significant appearance of the members of the Church triumphant in the spheres, the heavens reflected and will reflect forever their transcendent message, divinely written into them before history began. To see the universe truly was, for Dante, to know God through it. At one beautiful point in the *Paradiso*, he even asks us to look away from his lines of poetry toward the true source of their message:

> Lift up thine eyes with me then,
> reader, to the lofty wheels,
> directing them on that part where
> the one motion strikes the other,
> and from that point take thy
> pleasure in the art of the Master,
> who so loves it in His heart that
> His eye never leaves it.
> (10.7–12)

At another point, high in the heavens, looking back over the territory he has covered, the pilgrim gains a perspective of the Master's work such that the simple sight of it definitively brings home to him the limitations of earthbound desire:

> With my sight I returned through
> every one of the seven spheres, and
> I saw this globe such that I smiled
> at its paltry semblance; and that
> judgement which holds it for least I
> approve as best, and he whose
> thought is on other things may
> rightly be called just. I saw
> Latona's daughter glowing, without
> that shadow for which I once

believed her to be rare and dense;
thy son's aspect, Hyperion, I
endured there, and I saw how Maia
and Dione move in their circles near
him; from thence appeared to me the
tempering of Jove between his father
and his son, and from thence the
changes were clear to me which they
make in their positions; and all
seven showed me what is their
magnitude and what their speed and
at what distances their stations.
The little threshing-floor that
makes us so fierce all appeared to
me from hills to river-mouths, while
I was wheeling with the eternal
Twins. Then to the fair eyes I
turned my eyes again.

                                        (22.133–54)

This fairly lengthy passage is worth quoting in its entirety as an illustration of how Dante attempts to show us the inherent message that, whether or not it is read, is written into the universe and its wonders. In Dante's fiction, the pilgrim is simply reading with liberated eyes what is before us all, the reality of space manifesting God and drawing us toward the mind of which it is an expression.

God's "Other Book". In medieval tradition, the author of the Bible was ultimately God Himself, who inspired it as an account of providentially protected history from the beginning to the end of time. But God was said to have written another book as well, one He composed long before the Bible as His original act of Creation. The universe, in fact, because of the meaning that was said to be written into it, was God's "other book." Both books carried the message of God's eternal truth, both were allegorical, and the meaning of both inexhaustible. The same truth written into the crooked lines of time was spatially reflected by the universe. The great difference between the two works of the Creator was that man could obtain salvation only through the second, through the reading of scripture. This situation was the result of the Fall, which made necessary both the events of the New Testament and the scriptural account of them. That is, because man sinned, Christ's Incarnation became necessary as did our belief in it and in the revelations of the Bible.

The events of history from the Fall to the Second Coming were not a part of natural Creation, because of which it could not lead man to salvation. However, again according to tradition, Creation was originally presented to Adam and Eve as the clearly legible source of divine truth, as the book where they could read God's word and learn of His goodness. After the Fall, not only was the belief in the events of the Bible necessary to salvation, but Adam and Eve and their descendants lost the ability to see clearly God's signs in nature. It is important for our understanding of the *Paradiso* to be aware of the tradition that, before the Fall, the book of nature was clearly legible to man, as the revelation of God. In fact, in Dante's fiction, the pilgrim has revisited Eden and therefore his eyes must be reopened to the message so clearly written for the first man and woman. The pilgrim has graduated from understanding and reliving in Hell and Purgatory the events of the second book to the vision of truth in the original book. The reality and significance of history, so important to the composition of the first two *cantiche,* is replaced in the *Paradiso* by the universe's spatial message of divine truth, unfolded to the pilgrim during his voyage through the spheres.

A most significant moment in Dante's representation occurs in the *Primum Mobile,* at the edge of space. The pilgrim has a vision there of concentric circlings of ardent flames around a tiny and indescribably intense center of light. The circlings, which turn out to be the angels or spiritual movers of the physical spheres, match those of the material heavens in number and in their concentric conformation. The pilgrim senses that they are somehow the model for the universe itself. But he cannot understand why, unlike in the universe, the smaller the circlings are, the brighter and more swift they are. Beatrice's explanation is essentially that the difference is not in the message, but in the terms that express it. The nature of space is such that of necessity greatness is measured by size. Therefore, the immensity of the *Primum Mobile* is the physical expression of the power it reflects; its height above Earth, the apt image of its closeness to God. But, if we could bypass the terms inherent in the nature of space, the universe would be seen as revolving around God, not the Earth, and its greatest parts would be seen to be the closest to that spiritual center. The universe expresses physically the same thing the angels express spiritually, not the opposite, as it might appear to our sense-conditioned experience. The vision in the *Primum Mobile* is a revelation to the pilgrim's eyes of the ultimate message of Creation: that God, not the Earth, is at its center.

The natural philosophy of Dante's time was Aristotelian, treating the physical universe as interpretable by observation and experience. The universe was seen as a great scheme of causes and effects initiated at its circumference and reaching down to its immobile center, the Earth. But the thought of his day had long been nourished by the Platonic vision of an absolute center of being causing the existence around it of all other things. In other words, Dante's age had simultaneously a spiritual vision of God as the center of everything and a physical vision of the Earth as the center. Ironically, in later times, when the world was less certain of the centrality of the absolute, it developed, quite coincidentally, a new understanding of the physical universe in which the sun held a place of literal centrality. But Dante's picture of reality was Earth-centered and heaven-oriented. In the *Paradiso* he resolves this picture in semantic terms. That is, if we take "center" and "circumference" as spatial references, then the center is the smallest part, the circumference the greatest. But space itself is a language in which the greatness of the circumference is a sign, a way of communicating or externalizing a spiritual and inconceivable centrality.

The vision at the edge of space reveals the universe as the outward expression of its Maker, showing the pilgrim that, spiritually, it is outside of Him, not He outside of it. This vision represents a remarkable elaboration of the tradition of the allegory of God's "other book," showing that the relation of the angels' love to the physical motion it causes is ultimately allegorical. That is, the angels' love of God, their spiritual rotation around Him, not only moves the universe but is also the spirit of which the spheres are the letter. Dante's deeply medieval sense of the inalienable significance of reality led him beyond the interpretation of *reality* in the terms of *allegory*. The vision in the *Primum Mobile* is rather an interpretation of *allegory* in the terms of *reality*, for space itself is shown to be the model of all allegory, as well as of all language.

Expression. We are, I hope, beginning to see that the *Paradiso* is concerned on all levels with expression, understood by Dante as the mysterious relation between the intangible and the tangible. The spheres are physically moved by love, the parts of our body by our intentions. Similarly, we make gestures or speak audible words to give representation to feelings and experiences that only we can have. Verbal language is a highly conventional and uniquely human version of this mystery. Ultimately, our language is a temporal, man-made imitation of a universe of sensible signs expressing God's spiritual message. Expression, inseparable from significance, seems to be the universal principle on which the *Paradiso*'s poetic formula is based. The universe is imagined as anthropomorphically smiling and dancing its message of the order of its Maker's serene mind. This is Dante's way of stressing the inanimate spectacle of the world around us and above us as the expression of God and, as such, the model of all language. At the same time, Dante tries to show us disembodied expressiveness in the souls by letting them borrow the more essential, distilled language of the immortal stars. The souls, in fact, sparkle and rotate; they even form constellations; Beatrice eclipses. Dante tries to suggest an expressiveness beyond the senses through luminous imitation of the original, highest, and least material form of expression. The *Paradiso* explores all of reality as signifying a spiritual counterpart, whether that counterpart be the joy of an individual soul, or the mind of God, or a poet's vision.

Before leaving the subject, I would like to compare Dante's vision of the world to ours. Dante's vision is deeply medieval and most different from our modern way of thinking in its unshaken faith in the absolute and its attachment of significance to all things. His vision might seem to us dismissive of reality and even of language, for it attributes to everything the ulterior purpose of pointing to what we may not even believe in: the universe appears as a great system of signs pointing to God, our bodies are the means of expression for our souls. But, in his way, Dante's reverence for reality and for language greatly exceeds ours. In his thought, so different in this sense from Platonic thought, the physical world and the human body are not only real, they are indestructible, created by God to last forever. When he pictures all that exists in space or reaches us through the senses as pointing to a superior reality we cannot touch, far from denying outward reality, he is saying that, because it is real, it is significant. This may be as foreign to our way of seeing as Platonic thought would have been. In fact, while we value objective reality, we do not normally consider natural things to carry messages and we call superstitious those who do. But what cannot be foreign to us is Dante's profound assessment of our experience as inseparable from language. Like us, Dante is acutely aware that we are constantly reading signs. Like us, he perceives this reading as both conventional and subjective. Like much of the thought of our day, his interpretation of reality is ultimately an interpretation of language. However, unlike today, Dante has faith in unlimited meaning behind natural if not human language, and a religious sense of the sacredness of both.

The Final Vision. Against the background of the structure of God's original language written into the book of Creation, Dante represents the pilgrim's experience of reading messages mysteriously disembodied from their signs. Throughout the *Paradiso,* his poetic genius is constantly strained to formulate that "light" through the "shadows" of his images. We are made constantly aware of the poet's struggle to mediate between us and the supernatural impressions he himself cannot fully remember. The *Paradiso*'s poetics are based on the premise that the signs are not the reality, that the poet's words only point to what they cannot touch. But, paradoxically, the *Paradiso*'s poetics also depend on the reader's belief in those signs, on his belief that they express what they cannot express. In the simplest terms possible, Dante claims to have had the vision that only Saint Paul had had, an experience whose inexpressibility is stated by Saint Paul and admitted by Dante. But, unlike Saint Paul, who declined to speak of the unspeakable, Dante offers his poem as an example, as images of the unimaginable, as a monument, if not to the adequacy of signs, at least to their sacredness and divine origin. However, nothing in the *Paradiso* compares in its daring and its paradox to the conclusion of the final canto, where the poet recalls the pilgrim looking into the face of God. It is possible that there is no comparable moment in the history of Western literature.

The great Italian critic Benedetto Croce ridiculed the last canto with arguments that, in their way, were extremely perceptive. In essence, what Croce said was that Dante's final vision is a bluff, a trick played on the reader. Dante waves his poetic arms so vehemently toward the nonexistent vision that his reader may be convinced of its existence. Croce is right that God's face is not in Dante's poetry, and he is right that the poet's struggle dominates the last canto. But, if he truly believed that Dante's poetry failed him at the end, then it is his reading we must dismiss, certainly not the climax Dante's art reaches in the final moments of the *Divine Comedy*.

The images of the last canto, far from being rhetorically facile, point exactly where Dante wants them to point. They are images of their own failure, images of absence denoting presence somewhere else. The vision is gone. The signs left behind refer to that departure:

> From that moment my vision was
> greater than our speech, which fails
> at such a sight, and memory too
> fails at such excess. Like him that
> sees in a dream and after the dream
> the passion wrought by it remains
> and the rest returns not to his
> mind, such am I; for my vision
> almost wholly fades, and still there
> drops within my heart the sweetness

that was born of it. Thus the snow
loses its imprint in the sun; thus
in the wind on the light leaves the
Sibyl's oracle was lost.

(33.55–66)

Immediately after this beautiful passage, Dante plunges into the dramatic quest for the vision that consumed the pilgrim—and gave birth
to the poet. To give images to what he cannot even recover in his
memory seems, and is, a lost cause. But, just as the pilgrim once he
has fixed his eyes on the vision cannot avert them, so the poet cannot
yet let go of language. He tells us what he saw as he looked at God:
he saw all those things that are scattered and separate in the universe,
"bound together by love" in the divine conception of them; he saw
their perfection in that light itself of which everything else is a reflection; and he saw and comprehended the Trinitarian nature of God.
Just as the pilgrim did not avert his eyes from the overpowering vision
of the incomprehensible nature of God, so the poet finds an image,
that of three superimposed circles of the same size and yet each of a
different color. We are to visualize one circle simultaneously of three
different colors or, which is the same, three different circles, all the
same size and all in the same place. We cannot visualize what cannot
be visually, but neither can we understand the mystery of the Trinity.

The poet remembers that in these circles the greatest mystery of
all, the Incarnation, began to appear. He persists with one more image,
that of the squaring of the circle, or the geometrically impossible solution to the incompatibility of the curve and the straight line. Just as
the answer to this problem eludes the geometer no matter how hard
he tries to find it, so the pilgrim could not make out that deepest of
mysteries. Straining his memory to the utmost, Dante remembers
reaching in vain for the final incomprehensible truth. As the pilgrim
and the poet both stretch, equally hopelessly, toward the pilgrim's lost
vision, the distinction between Dante then and Dante now seems to
disappear. Dante remembers failing to see and simultaneously being
overpowered by a blast in which Christ made man was revealed to
him. "Here power failed the high phantasy" (33.142).

The conclusive ring of the fourth to last line, "*All'alta fantasia qui mancò possa*," cannot be adequately rendered in translation. The first words, suggesting the height to which the imagination has soared, and the last, declaring its failure, are divided by the word "*qui*" (here), which seems to be the limit at which the imagination was defeated. But where is "here"? Here on the page where the poet's struggle ended? The blast just described that annihilated the pilgrim? Whose phantasy, or imagination, failed? The pilgrim's into which the vision of Christ could not fit, or the poet's which could no longer find even inadequate images? Does the poet somehow retrieve, if not the pilgrim's vision, at least his simultaneous forgetting of it? Most important, is a shadow of the mystery of the Incarnation present in the poet's language, as incompatible to his vision as the divine nature is to the human body? If we could give specific answers to these questions, then Dante's poetry might have failed at the end, for it would have done no more than what language is designed to do, denote things within our experience.

The final canto is certainly, as Croce would tell us, a tour de force. But, except in the literal sense intended by Dante, it is not a failure. It does not express God, nor does it convince the reader that Dante saw God. But, by dramatizing the poet's imaginative quest toward the pilgrim's spiritual one, it produces a sense of something beyond images or signs. The pilgrim and the poet come together at a point where all imaginative power ends and which is somehow, if not the unimaginable, at least the border between it and the imaginable.

The story ends at this point, although there is still one *terzina* left in the poem: "but now my desire and will, like a wheel that spins with even motion, were revolved by the Love that moves the sun and the other stars" (33.143–45). The pilgrim is far away again, as the poet pronounces him integrated into the motion of divine love reflected by every natural thing.

Notes

1. John Freccero, "The Significance of *Terza Rima*," in *Dante: The Poetics of Conversion*, ed. Rachel Jacoff, 258–59 (Cambridge, Mass., and London, England: Harvard University Press, 1986).

2. Dante Alighieri, *La Vita Nuova*, trans. and intro. Barbara Reynolds (Bungay, Suffolk: Penguin, 1969), xlii.

3. Saint Augustine, *Confessions*, trans. R. S. Pine-Coffin (London, Reading, and Fakenham: Penguin Classics, 1969), 7:12:178. Further citations will be taken from this edition and documented in parentheses in the text.

4. Virgil, *The Aeneid*, trans. Robert Fitzgerald (New York: Random House, 1981), 6:870–86. Further citations will be taken from this edition and documented in parentheses in the text.

Bibliography

Primary Sources and Recommended Translations

Collected Works of Dante

The Portable Dante. Edited and with an introduction by Paolo Milano. Rev. ed. The Viking Library, Vol. 42. Hammondsworth: Penguin Books, 1978. Contains the excellent translation of the *Divine Comedy* by Laurence Binyon. This translation is the most subtle of the modern verse translations.

Works of Dante Alighieri. Translated and with a commentary by H. Oelsner, T. Okey, P. H. Wicksteed, and A. G. H. Howell. Temple Classics. London: J. M. Dent and Sons, Ltd., 1964. Good literal translation of all of Dante's works, with notes and commentary.

The Divine Comedy

The Divine Comedy. Translated by John Ciardi. New York: W. W. Norton and Co., 1977. Convenient one-volume edition with introduction and notes. A strong verse translation that, however, frequently distorts the original.

The Divine Comedy. Translated and with an introduction by Allen Mandelbaum and original drawings by Barry Moser. Berkeley, Los Angeles, and London: University of California Press, 1980–82. One of the best modern verse translations. Now available in paperback with notes. The publishers of the "California Dante" expect to present an accompanying volume of commentary for each *cantica*.

The Divine Comedy. Translated by Dorothy Sayers and Barbara Reynolds. New York: Penguin, 1949–1962. The translation of the *Inferno* and the

Bibliography

Purgatorio is by Dorothy Sayers, the *Paradiso* was completed by Barbara Reynolds after Sayers's death. This is not one of the best verse translations but the notes and introduction are particularly good.

The Divine Comedy. Translated by John D. Sinclair. 3 vols. New York: Oxford University Press, 1961. Excellent prose translation.

The Divine Comedy. Translated by Charles S. Singleton. 6 vols. Bollingen Series, 80. Princeton, N.J.: Princeton University Press, 1970–75. Detailed commentary. The literal prose translation is the best available, although not always as readable as Sinclair's.

The Divine Comedy. Translated by C. H. Sisson. Foreword to the American edition by T. G. Bergin; introduction, commentary, notes, and bibliography by David H. Higgins. Chicago: Reynery Gateway, 1981. Unrhymed verse translation designed to convey the meaning more literally.

Minor Works of Dante

Dante's Lyric Poetry. Translated and with a commentary by K. Foster and P. Boyde. 2 vols. Oxford: Clarendon Press, 1967.

Literary Criticism of Dante Alighieri. Translated and edited by Robert S. Haller. Lincoln: University of Nebraska Press, 1973. A collection of excerpts, in English translation, from Dante's works bearing on matters of literary criticism.

La Vita Nuova. Translated by Barbara Reynolds. New York: Penguin, 1969.

Monarchy and Three Political Letters. With an introduction by Donald Nicholl and a note on the chronology of Dante's political works by Colin Hardie. Westport, Connecticut: Hyperion Press, 1979.

A Translation of Dante's Eleven Letters. Translated by C. S. Latham. Edited by G. R. Carpenter. Boston: 1892.

Other Primary Sources

Augustine, Saint. *Confessions.* Translated by R. S. Pine-Coffin. London, Reading, and Fakenham: The Penguin Classics, 1961. Excellent translation with a short introduction.

Boethius. *The Consolation of Philosophy.* Translated and with an introduction and notes by Richard Green. The Library of Liberal Arts. Indianapolis and New York: The Bobbs-Merril Co., 1962.

Bonaventura, Saint. *The Mind's Road to God.* Translated by George Boas. The Library of Liberal Arts. Indianapolis, New York, and Kansas City: The Bobbs-Merrill Co., 1953. A short work by a near contemporary of

Dante's whose philosophical background is close to Dante's. Introduction and bibliography are included.

Smith, James Robinson, trans. *The Earliest Lives of Dante.* The Library of Liberal Arts. New York: Indianapolis and New York: The Bobbs-Merrill Co., 1968. Translation of Giovanni Boccaccio's and Leonardo Bruni's lives of Dante.

Virgil. *The Aeneid.* Translated by Robert Fitzgerald. New York: Random House, 1981. This translation is strongly recommended.

Secondary Sources

Books

Asin Palacios, Miguel. *Islam and the "Divine Comedy."* Translated and abridged by Harold Sutherland. New York: Barnes and Noble, 1968. On the probability of the transmission of Islamic models to Dante.

Auerbach, Erich, *Scenes from the Drama of European Literature: Six Essays.* Translated by Ralph Manheim, Catherine Garvin, and Erich Auerbach. New York: Meridian Books, 1959. This collection contains two of Auerbach's most famous essays on Dante: "Figura" and "St. Francis of Assisi in Dante's *Commedia.*"

————. *Dante: Poet of the Secular World.* Translated by Ralph Manheim. Chicago: University of Chicago Press, 1961.

Barbi, Michele. *Life of Dante.* Edited and translated by P. Ruggiers. Berkeley: University of California, 1960.

Bernardo, Aldo S., and Anthony L. Pellegrini. *A Critical Study Guide to Dante's "Divine Comedy."* Totowa, N. J.: Littlefield, Adams and Co., in association with Education Research Associates, Inc., of America, Philadelphia, 1968. Contains visual aids, summaries, biography, bibliography, etc.

Bloom, Harold, editor. *Dante,* in *Modern Critical Views.* New York, New Haven, and Philadelphia: Chelsea House, 1986.

Brieger, Peter, Millard Meiss, and Charles S. Singleton. *Illuminated Manuscripts of the "Divine Comedy."* Bollingen Series, 81. Princeton, N. J.: Princeton University Press, 1969. A beautiful presentation in two volumes, one of text and one of plates, of over 1,000 miniatures from the medieval manuscripts of the poem.

Bibliography

Charity, A. C. *Events and Their Afterlife: The Dialectics of Christian Typology in the Bible and Dante.* Cambridge: Cambridge University Press, 1966. The first part is an excellent study of biblical exegesis. The second part deals with Dante, especially the Cacciaguida episode, in the context of biblical exegesis.

Cosmo, Umberto. *A Handbook to Dante Studies.* Translated by David Moore. Oxford: Blackwell, 1950.

Davis, Charles Till. *Dante and the Idea of Rome.* Oxford: Clarendon Press, 1957. Excellent detailed study of the background of Dante's view of the Roman Empire.

————. *Dante's Italy and Other Essays.* Philadelphia: University of Pennsylvania, 1984.

Demaray, John G. *The Invention of Dante's "Commedia."* New Haven, Conn., and London: Yale University Press, 1974. An informative book about pilgrimages in Dante's times and their relevance to the imagery of the traveller in the *Divine Comedy.*

D'Entrèves, A. P. *Dante as Political Thinker.* Oxford: Clarendon Press, 1955.

Foster, Kenelm, O. P. *God's Tree.* London: Darton, Longman and Todd, 1957.

————. *The Two Dantes and Other Studies.* London: Darton, Longman and Todd, 1977.

Freccero, John. *Dante: The Poetics of Conversion.* Edited and with an introduction by Rachel Jacoff. Cambridge, Mass., and London: Harvard University Press, 1986.

————, editor. *Dante: A Collection of Critical Essays.* Englewood Cliffs, N. J.: Prentice-Hall, 1965. A collection of essays noteworthy in different ways. Special attention should be paid to the essay by Bruno Nardi, one of the great Dante scholars of our times but also one whose work is rarely available in English; to Robert Kaske's exemplary exegesis; and to Renato Poggioli's provocative reading of the Francesca episode.

Gardner, Edmond G. *Dante's Ten Heavens.* London: J. M. Dent and Sons, 1904. Informative presentation of traditional material relevant to the background of the *Paradiso.*

————. *Dante and the Mystics.* London and New York: J. M. Dent and Sons, 1968. Survey of mystical writers whose works are reflected in the *Divine Comedy.*

Giamatti, A. B., editor. *Dante in America: The First Two Centuries.* Medieval and Renaissance Texts and Studies, vol. 23. Binghamton, N.Y.: Medieval and Renaissance Texts and Studies, 1983. A collection of nineteenth- and twentieth-century essays by well-known Americans.

Gilson, Etienne. *Dante and Philosophy.* Translated by David Moore. New York: Harper & Row, 1963.

Grandgent, Charles H. *Companion to the "Divine Comedy."* Edited by Charles S. Singleton. Cambridge, Mass.: Harvard University Press, 1975.

Hollander, Robert. *Allegory in Dante's "Commedia."* Princeton, N. J.: Princeton University Press, 1969.

―――. *Studies in Dante.* Ravenna: Longo Editore, 1980.

Holmes, George. *Dante.* Oxford, Toronto, and Melbourne: Oxford University Press, 1980.

Kay, Richard. *Dante's Swift and Strong: Essays on Inferno XV.* Lawrence: The Regents Press of Kansas, 1978. Challenges traditional interpretation of the Brunetto Latini episode.

Mazzeo, Joseph Anthony. *Structure and Thought in the "Paradiso."* Ithaca, N. Y.: Cornell University Press, 1958. Informative presentation of philosophical background. Oversimplified discussion of Dante's Platonism.

―――. *Medieval Cultural Tradition in Dante's "Comedy."* Ithaca, N. Y.: Cornell University Press, 1960. Useful presentation of background material, especially concerning light metaphysics.

Mazzotta, Giuseppe. *Dante Poet of the Desert: History and Allegory in the "Divine Comedy."* Princeton, N. J.: Princeton University Press, 1979. Theoretical discussion of Dante's poetics.

Moore, Edward. *Studies in Dante.* Four series. Oxford: 1896–1917. Thorough study of Dante's sources.

Quinones, Ricardo J. *Dante Alighieri.* Twayne's World Authors Series, 563. Boston: Twayne Publishers, 1979.

Reade, W. H. V. *The Moral System of Dante's "Inferno."* Port Washington, N. Y., London: Kennikat Press, 1909. Very good but very technical discussion of the division of the sinners in Hell.

Schnapp, Jeffrey T. *The Transfiguration of History at the Center of Dante's "Paradise."* Princeton, N. J.: Princeton University Press, 1986. Scholarly and sensitive study of the heaven of Mars in the light of biblical and iconographic tradition.

Singleton, Charles S. *Dante Studies I: "Commedia": Elements of Structure.* Cambridge, Mass.: Harvard University Press, 1954. Revolutionary discussion of Dante's allegory and of his presentation of history.

―――. *Dante Studies II: Journey to Beatrice.* Cambridge, Mass.: Harvard University Press, 1958. Important study of the *Purgatorio's* Eden cantos.

Thompson, David. *Dante's Epic Journeys.* Baltimore and London: Johns Hopkins University Press, 1974. Useful and readable discussion of Dante's use of the Homeric and Virgilian traditions.

Toynbee, Paget. *Dante Alighieri: His Life and Works.* Reedited with an introduction and notes by Charles S. Singleton. New York: Harper & Row, 1965.

Bibliography

——. *Dante Dictionary.* Rev. ed. Edited by Charles S. Singleton. Oxford: Clarendon Press, 1965. Original title: *A Dictionary of Proper Names and Notable Matters in the Works of Dante.* Oxford: 1898. Invaluable tool for the student of Dante.

Articles

Many of the best-known articles on Dante are included in the several anthologies listed above. See Bloom, Freccero, Giamatti.

Robert Ball, "Theological Semantics: Virgil's *Pietas* and Dante's *Pietà.*" *Stanford Italian Review* 2 (1981):59–79.

Chiarenza, Marguerite. "Boethian Themes in Dante's Reading of Virgil." *Stanford Italian Review* 3 (1983):25–35.

——. "Time and Eternity in the Myths of *Paradiso* XVII." In *Dante, Petrarch and Others: Studies in the Italian Trecento. Essays in Honor of Charles Singleton,* edited by Aldo S. Bernardo and Anthony L. Pellegrini, 133–51. Binghamton, N. Y.: Medieval and Renaissance Texts and Studies, 1983.

Fitzgerald, Robert, "Generations of Leaves." *Perspectives U.S.A.* 8 (1954):68–85.

——. "The Style that Does Honor." *Kenyon Review* 14 (1952):278–285.

Hardie, Colin Graham. "Cacciaguida's Prophecy in *Paradiso* XVII." *Traditio* 19 (1963):167–94. Excellent study of the political details of the prophecy.

Kaske, R. E. "Dante's *Purgatorio* XXXII and XXXIII: A Survey of Christian History." *University of Toronto Quarterly* 43 (1974):193–214.

——. "The Seven *Status Ecclesiae* in *Purgatorio* XXXII–XXXIII." In *Dante, Petrarch and Others: Studies in the Italian Trecento. Essays in Honor of Charles Singleton,* edited by Aldo S. Bernardo and Anthony L. Pellegrini, 89–113. Binghamton, N. Y.: Medieval and Renaissance Texts and Studies, 1983.

Longen, Eugene M. "The Grammar of Apotheosis: *Paradiso* XXXIII, 94–99." *Dante Studies* 93 (1975):209–14.

Murtaugh, Daniel M. " '*Figurando il paradiso*': The Signs that Render Dante's Heaven." *PMLA* 90 (1975):277–84. On the poetics of the *Paradiso.*

Olson, P. R. "Theme and Structure in the Exordium of the *Paradiso.*" *Italica* 39 (1962):89–104. Points out Aristotelian and Platonic themes that, already present in the first *terzina* of the *Paradiso,* pervade the whole *cantica.*

Peterson, Mark A. "Dante and the 3-Sphere." *American Journal of Physics* 47 (1981):1031–35. Finds in Dante an entirely original conception of the universe not understood in Dante's day but compatible with twentieth-century cosmology.

Ransom, Daniel J. "*Panis Angelorum*: A Palinode in the *Paradiso.*" *Dante Studies* 95 (1977):81–94.

Spitzer, Leo. "The Addresses to the Reader in the *Commedia.*" *Italica* 32 (1955):143–65.

Bibliographies

Koch, Theodore W. *Catalogue of the Dante Collection Presented by Willard Fiske to Cornell University.* 2 vols. and supplements. Ithaca, N. Y.: Cornell University Press, 1898–1921. The standard bibliography of printed works on Dante.

Dante Studies with the Annual Report of the Dante Society. This excellent journal of Dante studies contains an annual critical bibliography.

See also Cosmo, *A Handbook to Dante Studies.*

Index

Adam, 29, 34, 59, 60, 61, 62, 72, 87, 119
Adrian V, Pope, 68
Aeneas, 24, 25, 44, 45, 46, 47, 79, 80, 83, 100, 105, 108
allegory, 9, 10, 11, 13, 33, 56–59, 117, 121
Anchises, 24, 25, 45, 80, 83, 105, 106
Aristotle, 8, 54
    Aristotelian, 75, 120
Auerbach, Erich, 14
Augustan, 24, 25
Augustine, St., 4, 13, 14, 63, 77, 84–86, 110, 111
    Augustinian, 55, 64, 85
    Confessions, 85
Augustus, 23, 24, 52, 79

Beatrice, 5, 19–21, 22, 23, 28, 33, 37, 58, 66, 70, 81–89, 90, 93–99, 101, 102, 104, 113, 114, 115, 116, 119, 121
Bible, 13, 56, 57, 58, 70, 118, 119
    Old Testament, 57, 81
    New Testament, 57, 81, 119
    Scripture, 13, 57, 58, 81, 110, 119
Boethius, 4, 65, 109
    Boethian, 64
    Consolation of Philosophy, 109

Boniface VIII, Pope, 12
Brunetto Latini, 4, 41–43, 48, 105

Cacciaguida, 3, 105–8, 109, 110
Caesar, 52, 53, 59, 60
Cato, 59–62
Cavalcanti, Cavalcante, 38–41
Cavalcanti, Guido, 39, 40, 41, 69
Christ, 24, 26, 31, 35, 46, 50, 51, 52, 53, 56, 57, 58, 61, 62, 70, 72, 73, 74, 75, 77, 78, 79, 81, 82, 83, 85, 86, 87, 88, 90, 100, 110, 114, 119, 124, 125
Christian, 12, 35, 43, 46, 51, 55, 56, 60, 61, 63, 70, 71, 73, 74, 78, 79, 82, 86, 88, 107, 108, 110
    Christianity, 26, 30, 46, 79, 81, 87, 100
Church, 12, 24, 39, 52, 70, 81, 102, 103, 116, 117
Convivio, 47, 93
Creation, 7, 13, 28, 37, 43, 58, 81, 94, 97, 98, 99, 118, 119, 120, 122
Croce, Benedetto, 11, 123, 125

Dido, 25, 45, 83, 85
Dominic, St., 103

Eagle, 104, 114

Eden, 19, 62, 86–89, 101, 102, 119
Empire, 3, 23, 24, 52, 70, 79, 100, 104
Empyrean, 19, 52, 95, 110, 115, 116
Epicurus, 39
Eve, 59, 60, 119

Farinata, 11, 38–41, 48, 105
Florence, 2, 3, 4, 40, 105
Florentine, 3, 39
Francesca da Rimini, 7, 11, 34, 35–38, 48, 49, 50, 77
Francis, St., 43, 103
Freccero, John, 12, 13, 14, 15, 55

Ghibelline, 3, 12, 39
Giotto, 4, 69
gods, 24, 25, 44, 45, 70, 79, 81, 83
Golden Age, 78, 88
Griffin, 81
Guelfs, 2, 3, 39
Guido da Montefeltro, 43

heavens, 19, 54, 94, 97, 100, 102, 103, 110, 114, 117, 119
Hemisphere, 19, 31, 44, 54, 59, 60, 89
    Northern, 54, 59
    Southern, 19, 44, 54
Henry VII, Emperor, 3
Homer, 43, 44, 46
    Homeric, 44, 46

Incarnation, 96, 119, 124
Italy, 2, 3, 4, 5, 14, 24, 26, 44, 45, 71, 79

Judgment (Day), 68, 81, 82, 88, 102
Jupiter, 24, 79, 104

Limbo, 30, 31, 81, 84
Lucy, St., 23, 28, 66

Marcellus, 80, 83
Mars (heaven of), 105, 107, 114
Matelda, 87, 88
Mercury (heaven of), 113
Montaperti, 39, 40
Moon, 94, 97, 102

pagan, 59, 60, 61, 70, 74, 78, 83, 86
paganism, 74
Paolo, 35–38, 49, 50
Paul, St., 100, 101, 108, 110–12, 123
Pauline, 100, 110, 111
Platonic, 120, 122
Pope, 2, 3, 12, 52
Papacy, 3, 68
Primum Mobile, 94, 95, 119, 120, 121
Prologue (scene), 22, 23, 33, 45, 87
prophecy, 26, 78, 79, 106, 107, 110
Providence, 26, 46, 58, 70, 81, 103, 105, 107, 108–10

Ruggieri (Archbishop), 48, 51

Satan, 51–55, 89, 90
Singleton, Charles, 12, 13, 14, 15, 22
Siren, 66, 67
Sordello, 69–72, 74, 75
spheres, 19, 94, 116, 117, 119, 121
Statius, 69, 71, 72–78, 79, 90, 91
Stoic, 25, 60, 61, 80
Stoicism, 25, 59, 81

Thomas, St., 103
    Thomistic, 63, 64
Trojan, 24, 44, 45, 46, 47, 79
    Horse, 44, 45, 46
    War, 44, 47, 79

Index

Ugolino, 48–51

Ulysses, 11, 24, 43–48, 67

universe, 19, 31, 53, 54, 89, 90, 95,
    97, 98, 101, 110, 112, 114,
    115, 116–22, 124

Virgil, 23–27, 28, 31, 32, 33, 34,
35, 38, 40, 44, 45, 46, 53, 54,
55, 56, 58, 59, 60, 64, 66, 67,
    69–89, 91, 100, 110
    Aeneid, 24, 25, 26, 44, 70, 73,
    75, 76, 78, 79–81, 83
    Fourth Eclogue, 78, 79

Vita Nuova, 20, 21, 82, 85

About the Author

Born in the United States, Marguerite Mills Chiarenza began her studies of Dante and Latin literature in high school, in the Classical Lyceum in Florence, Italy. She did her undergraduate work at the University of Rome, where she had the opportunity to study under well-known Italian classicists and medievalists. She received her Ph.D. from Cornell in 1970 and since then has published a series of articles on different aspects of Dante's relation to classical literature and of his poetics, especially in the *Paradiso*. She is now an associate professor at the University of British Columbia, where she has taught Dante for seventeen years.

ISBN 0-8057-7985-X